BARRON'S

S0-AJV-891

CHARLOTTE BRONTË'S

Jane Eyre

BY

Joyce Milton

SERIES EDITOR

Michael Spring
Editor, *Literary Cavalcade*
Scholastic Inc.

BARRON'S

BARRON'S EDUCATIONAL SERIES, INC.

Woodbury, New York / London / Toronto / Sydney

ACKNOWLEDGMENTS

We would like to acknowledge the many painstaking hours of work Holly Hughes and Thomas F. Hirsch have devoted to the making the *Book Notes* series a success.

© Copyright 1984 by Barron's Educational Series, Inc.

All inquiries should be addressed to:
Barron's Educational Series, Inc.
113 Crossways Park Drive
Woodbury, New York 11797

Library of Congress Catalog Card No. 84-18435

International Standard Book No. 0-8120-3422-8

Library of Congress Cataloging in Publication Data
Milton, Joyce.
    Charlotte Brontë's Jane Eyre.

    (Barron's book notes)
    Bibliography: p. 111
    Summary: A guide to reading "Jane Eyre" with a critical
and appreciative mind. Includes background on the
author's life and times, sample tests, term paper suggestions, and a reading list.
    1. Brontë, Charlotte, 1816–1855. Jane Eyre.
[1. Brontë, Charlotte, 1816–1855. Jane Eyre. 2. English
literature—History and criticism] I. Title. II. Series.
PR4167.J5M54 1984   823'.8   84-18435
ISBN 0-8120-3422-8 (pbk.)

PRINTED IN THE UNITED STATES OF AMERICA

456   550   987654321

CONTENTS

ADVISORY BOARD

HOW TO USE THIS BOOK

You have to know how to approach literature in order to get the most out of it. This *Barron's Book Notes* volume follows a plan based on methods used by some of the best students to read a work of literature.

Begin with the guide's section on the author's life and times. As you read, try to form a clear picture of the author's personality, circumstances, and motives for writing the work. This background usually will make it easier for you to hear the author's tone of voice, and follow where the author is heading.

Then go over the rest of the introductory material—such sections as those on the plot, characters, setting, themes, and style of the work. Underline, or write down in your notebook, particular things to watch for, such as contrasts between characters and repeated literary devices. At this point, you may want to develop a system of symbols to use in marking your text as you read. (Of course, you should only mark up a book you own, not one that belongs to another person or a school.) Perhaps you will want to use a different letter for each character's name, a different number for each major theme of the book, a different color for each important symbol or literary device. Be prepared to mark up the pages of your book as you read. Put your marks in the margins so you can find them again easily.

Now comes the moment you've been waiting for—the time to start reading the work of literature. You may want to put aside your *Barron's Book Notes* volume until you've read the work all the way through. Or you may want to alternate, reading the *Book Notes* analysis of each section as soon as you have finished reading the corresponding part of the original. Before you move on, reread crucial passages you don't fully understand. (Don't take this guide's analysis for granted—make up your own mind as to what the work means.)

Once you've finished the whole work of literature, you may want to review it right away, so you can firm up your ideas about what it means. You may want to leaf through the book concentrating on passages you marked in reference to one character or one theme. This is also a good time to reread the *Book Notes* introductory material, which pulls together insights on specific topics.

When it comes time to prepare for a test or to write a paper, you'll already have formed ideas about the work. You'll be able to go back through it, refreshing your memory as to the author's exact words and perspective, so that you can support your opinions with evidence drawn straight from the work. Patterns will emerge, and ideas will fall into place; your essay question or term paper will almost write itself. Give yourself a dry run with one of the sample tests in the guide. These tests present both multiple-choice and essay questions. An accompanying section gives answers to the multiple-choice questions as well as suggestions for writing the essays. If you have to select a term paper topic, you may choose one from the list of suggestions in this book. This guide also provides you with a reading list, to help you when you start research for a term paper, and a selection of provocative comments by critics, to spark your thinking before you write.

THE AUTHOR AND HER TIMES

Charlotte Brontë is one of those authors whose life has attracted as much attention as her writing. Charlotte and her family have been the subject of many books, a stage play, and a film by the French director Truffaut. For some people, interest in the Brontë family is almost on the level of a cult, and there are even organized tours to the places associated with the family's history.

At first glance, you may wonder what all the fuss is about. Born in 1816, Charlotte was one of six children of a country preacher. She lived a quiet, uneventful life. Except for a few years away at school and several brief stints as a teacher, she spent most of her time at home. The Brontë family as a whole suffered from poor health and all of the children died relatively young; but that in itself wasn't unusual in the middle of the nineteenth century. In fact, the only truly unusual events of Charlotte's life occurred during the months between October of 1847 and June of 1848 when she and her two surviving sisters, Emily and Anne, emerged quite suddenly as successful novelists.

At the time, literary society in England was a very small world. For a complete unknown to publish a successful novel was relatively unusual. For three unknowns to manage it in a single year was unheard of. Naturally, everyone was curious about them, though normally the curiosity would have died down as soon as a new subject for gossip came along. But an aura of mystery surrounding the identity of the Brontës kept them a subject of interest for much longer than that. In all innocence, the three sisters had chosen to publish their books under male pen names—as Currer (Charlotte), Acton (Anne), and Ellis (Emily) Bell. They did this partly to escape the prejudice against women novelists and partly to avoid embarrassing friends and acquaintances who might find themselves portrayed in the novels. As it turned out, the pen names only helped to make the Brontës more famous. Everyone was wildly eager to figure out the true identities of Currer, Acton, and Ellis Bell. Were they really men? Or if they were women, why were they pretending to be men? There was even a rumor, encouraged by Emily and Anne's publisher, that the three authors were one and the same person.

By the time the truth became widely known, Emily and Anne were dead. Charlotte was the only Brontë who became a literary celebrity during her own lifetime, but all three sisters were well on their way to becoming cult heroines.

Unlike many writers who achieve instant fame, the Brontës' books have stood the test of time. Two of the three books published during that ten-month period in 1847-48—Charlotte's *Jane Eyre* and Emily's *Wuthering Heights*—are still widely read and enjoyed today. Anne's novel, *Agnes Grey*, has never been as popular, but its admirers are often the most enthusiastic of all. One highly respected critic even called it "the most perfect narrative in English prose."

Precisely because the Brontës led such limited lives, many readers have been quick to jump to the conclusion that their novels are highly autobiographical. Where would three young women—who had done little traveling and knew only a few people—get their material, if not out of their own lives? Trying to reconstruct Charlotte Brontë's private life from scenes in her books has become almost a game.

It's true that Charlotte Brontë, like all writers, borrowed from her own experiences. But it's a mistake to think that Charlotte Brontë *was* Jane Eyre. There are almost as many differences between Charlotte and her famous heroine as there are likenessess. For one thing, Jane Eyre finds her happiness only through love and marriage. The real Charlotte Brontë found her fulfillment in her dedication to writing.

There are other differences, too. Jane Eyre is an unloved orphan. But Charlotte Brontë, although her mother died when she was only five, had a father, a loving aunt, and older sisters to care for her. We don't know very much about Charlotte's relationship with her father. Some biographers think that he was cold and eccentric. Others say that he was a domineering man who did his best to make sure his daughters wouldn't become independent enough to marry and leave home. But no one can be sure if either of these theories is true.

In 1824, eight-year-old Charlotte and her sister Emily joined their two older sisters at Cowan Bridge, a school for the daughters of clergymen. Many readers of *Jane Eyre* have wondered whether Cowan Bridge was really as terrible as Lowood, the school described in the novel. Charlotte Brontë apparently thought it was, although some former pupils of Cowan Bridge later came forward in its defense. One thing we know for sure is that the teachers at Cowan Bridge were in no hurry to contact parents when their pupils fell ill. Both of Charlotte's older sisters, Maria and Elizabeth, came down with tuberculosis in 1825, and by the time the school notified Mr. Brontë, the girls were gravely ill. Maria died a few days after her return home, Elizabeth a few months later.

After this double tragedy, the surviving Brontë children were kept at home, where they were taught by their Aunt Branwell. In their free time, the three sisters and their brother, also called Branwell (it was his middle name) invented complicated fantasies and produced tiny, handwritten books. Many children still indulge in this form of make-believe, but writing down one's own fantasies was far more common in the days when children had fewer books and no television to entertain them. What made the Brontës unusual was that for them the world of make-believe became more important than anything else. Emily and Anne were mainly involved in writing stories about an imaginary island in the Pacific, called Gondal. Charlotte and her brother concentrated on spinning tales about Angria, a fantasy kingdom in West Africa populated by immigrants from England and France. Charlotte was in her mid-twenties before she finally gave up creating new episodes in the lives of these imaginary characters.

In 1830, Mr. Brontë fell ill. Ironically, since he recovered to live to an advanced age, the lives of his three daughters were made miserable from that time on by the fear that their father would die and they would be left to support themselves. (Even more ironically, Mr. Brontë outlived all his children.) The next year, Charlotte was sent to school again. Roe Head, as the school was called, was a very pleasant place, not at all like Cowan Bridge. While Charlotte was an excellent student and made two lifelong friends during her two years at Roe Head, she was too shy to feel completely at ease in unfamiliar surroundings. After leaving school in 1832, at the age of sixteen, she spent most of the next ten years at home. The only exceptions were a two-and-a-half-year period when she went back to Roe Head as a teacher while first Emily and then Anne were pupils there, and two brief stints as a governess that lasted only about ten months altogether.

Unlike her sister Emily, who never tired of hiking the windswept moors around the Brontë home in Yorkshire, Charlotte longed for travel and a more active life. Since her experiences as a governess had been unhappy ones, she decided that perhaps she and Emily should open a school of their own. Her plan called for them to prepare by going to Belgium to brush up on their knowledge of foreign languages. Charlotte was already twenty-six when she and her sister entered the school of Monsieur and Madame Héger in Brussels, and she was soon teaching English lessons as well as studying. Emily went home after a year, but Charlotte stayed on until 1843, when for some reason the relationship between herself and Mme Héger became tense. Judging from some letters she wrote, it seems that Charlotte had fallen in love with M. Héger. Had he returned her affection? Probably not. The theme of an impossible love affair—with a married man, a teacher, in one case even a Belgian teacher—keeps coming up in Charlotte Brontë's novels. Many readers can't help concluding from this that M. Héger was the great passion of Charlotte's life. But we can't be sure.

Less than two years after Charlotte's return home, her brother Branwell was involved in a scandal. As the only boy, Branwell had been the focus of the whole family's hopes for worldly success. Charlotte, in particular, had always believed that her brother was the true genius of the family. The devoted sister was the last to see what was obvious to everyone else:

Branwell was a total failure. Not only had he never carried through on his ambition to become a painter, he was an alcoholic, a gambler, and eventually a drug addict. Anne, the only sister who had managed to persevere with her career as a governess, had arranged a job for Branwell as a tutor with the same family she worked for. Branwell repaid the favor by getting involved in a messy affair with the lady of the house, Mrs. Robinson. In the end, both he and Anne were sent away in disgrace.

By 1845, it seemed that all of the Brontës' hopes and plans had come to nothing. Branwell was an idle drunk, whose periodic rampages disrupted the peace of the house. Charlotte and Emily's school never got past the planning stage, and all three sisters were at home again. Only then, as a last resort, did the Brontë women begin to think seriously about writing for publication. *Jane Eyre* was actually Charlotte's second novel (her first, *The Professor*, wasn't published till years later), but it came out before either of her sisters' books and paved the way for their success. Some critics have a hard time understanding how Charlotte, many of whose childhood Angria stories are quite awful, could have developed into the mature writer who produced *Jane Eyre*. However, in one way there is a direct connection between those private childhood fantasies and *Jane Eyre:* Unlike most writers of her time, Charlotte didn't claim to be presenting an objective view of society. And she could identify with people who were the outsiders in Victorian society—children, poor relatives, powerless employees of rich families, women in love with men who did not—or could not—love them in return. Today it's quite common for a novel to be intensely personal. In 1847, when *Jane Eyre* appeared, it was a daring departure, perhaps more daring than even Charlotte realized.

Charlotte's naivete about literary society is shown by an incident that occurred shortly after *Jane Eyre* was published. William Thackeray, a successful and socially prominent novelist, wrote Charlotte a letter praising her book, and in gratitude she dedicated the second edition to him. Charlotte may have been the only literary person in England who didn't know that Thackeray, like Mr. Rochester in *Jane Eyre*, had a wife who was insane. To make matters worse, Thackeray had just published a novel about a scheming governess who tries to seduce her employer. Gossips put two and two together and decided that the author of *Jane Eyre* had been having an affair with Thackeray!

As this incident shows, women novelists in the 19th century were expected to be personalities—either romantic adventuresses or eccentrics. Charlotte confounded everyone by being neither. She impressed the people who met her as being small, ordinary-looking, and rather shy. Nor, despite the passionate pleas for women's independence in her books, was she much interested in becoming a feminist crusader. All she did, or wanted to do, was to write good books. Instead of giving up in disappointment, some of her admirers became all the more curious and continued to pick through Charlotte's novels in search of clues to hidden mysteries in her past.

In 1854, Charlotte did the one thing that could have surprised her intimate friends and her public alike—she got married! Charlotte had received two marriage proposals when she was in her twenties—one from a man she barely knew and another from a clergyman who made no secret of the fact that he was proposing on the rebound after being rejected by another young woman—but she had always taken it for granted that she would never marry. How could she hope to find a husband who'd understand her need to write or who'd measure up to the romantic heroes of her imagination? Oddly enough the man Charlotte finally chose to wed was neither her literary equal nor a brooding hero in the mold of *Jane Eyre's* Mr. Rochester. He was Arthur Bell Nicholls, a sober curate (assistant minister) who had been quietly in love with Charlotte for several years before he even knew that she was the author of the celebrated novel, *Jane Eyre*. Though not an intellectual himself, Bell was apparently quite proud to discover that the quiet middle-aged woman he had fallen in love with was a literary genius. And Charlotte, to the dismay and skepticism of some of her admirers, had decided that she could combine a career as the author of unconventional novels with a very conventional married life.

Charlotte seemed about to do just that. She was already pregnant when, after less than a year of marriage, she fell ill and died of tuberculosis—the same disease that had killed her sisters and brother.

Charlotte's early death provided the drama that many of her readers had looked for, and failed to find, in her life. Some biographers have portrayed Charlotte as a tragic heroine, who walked around shrouded by an aura of gloom, constantly preoccupied by the subject of death. But when you consider the number of early deaths in her family, it's surprising that Charlotte worried as little about death as she did. In spite of her withdrawn, introspective childhood, Charlotte managed to lead a productive and fulfilled life. She completed four novels, coped with the stress of sudden fame, and at the age of thirty-eight decided to embark on a career as a wife and mother. According to her biographer and friend, Mrs. Gaskell (see the Further Reading section of this guide), Charlotte Brontë refused to believe, almost to the end of her last illness, that she was going to suffer the same fate as her four sisters and her brother. When she heard her husband at her bedside praying to God to spare her life, Charlotte's reaction was surprise. "Oh, I am not going to die, am I?" she asked. "He will not separate us; we have been so happy."

THE NOVEL

The Plot

Jane Eyre is the story of a poor, orphaned girl's search for love. In the first part of the novel, Jane is ten years old and living, none too happily, at Gateshead House with Mrs. Reed, her uncle's widow, and the three Reed children—Eliza, Georgiana, and John. John is a bully, and when Jane fights back after he throws a book at her head, Mrs. Reed blames her for starting the fight and lying about it. As punishment, Jane is shut up in an empty bedroom—called the red-room, where she has a terrifying experience that she interprets as a visitation from the ghost of her dead Uncle Reed. A few months later, Mrs. Reed turns Jane over to a gloomy death-obsessed clergyman, Mr. Brocklehurst, who runs a charity school for the daughters of poor churchmen. She tells him to watch Jane carefully, because the girl is a liar.

Lowood, the charity boarding school, is a dismal place. There is never enough to eat, and the girls are forbidden even the smallest pleasures in the name of teaching them Christian humility. Jane makes friends with a sweet-natured, pious girl named Helen Burns, who tells her that they ought to bear their sufferings at the school with patience. Helen never shows resentment, even when she becomes the favorite target of the school's nastiest teacher, Miss Scatcherd. But when Mr. Brocklehurst humiliates Jane by repeating Mrs. Reed's charge against her in front of the whole school, she rebels. She talks the school superintendent into getting a letter from the Reed family apothecary (who treated Jane after her ordeal in the red-room), which clears her name.

When spring comes, the school is swept by a typhus epidemic. About half the girls fall ill, and some even die. Helen, too, is ill, but from consumption (tuberculosis). When Jane sneaks into Helen's room for a visit, she is shocked to find her friend has only a few hours to live. Helen dies in Jane's arms, proclaiming her steadfast faith in God.

As a result of the epidemic, Lowood comes under investigation, and conditions at the school are improved. Jane stays on, as a pupil and later as a teacher, until she is nineteen years old. Jane has become a dear friend of Miss Temple, the school superintendent, and when she leaves her job to get married, Jane decides that the time has come for her to leave as well.

Jane is hired as a governess by a Mrs. Fairfax, who lives in a substantial but rather gloomy country man-or-house, Thornfield Hall. Only after she has moved in does Jane realize that Mrs. Fairfax is only the house-keeper. Jane becomes quite fond of her only pupil, a saucy little French girl named Adèle Varens. Yet there is an aura of mystery about the house—the master, Mr. Edward Rochester, is seldom at home, and from time to time Jane hears eerie laughter coming from one of the locked rooms on the third story of the house. Mrs. Fairfax tells her that this is Grace Poole, an otherwise taciturn servant who spends much of her time sewing in that part of the house.

One wintry night, Mr. Rochester returns unexpectedly to Thornfield. He is a dark, brooding man in his late thirties, with an abrupt, imperious manner. Jane first meets him on the road, after he's been thrown from his horse, and offers him help without realizing who he is. Later, back at Thornfield, when Rochester asks her if she thinks he's handsome, Jane is outspoken enough to say, truthfully, "No, sir." Instead of being offended, Rochester is intrigued and charmed by the boldness of the new governess. There is already a rapport developing between the two of them when, one night, Jane awakens to the sound of the eerie laugh just outside her bedroom door, smells smoke, and discovers that someone has set fire to the hangings around Mr. Rochester's bed. She douses the flames with a pitcher of water. The way Rochester holds Jane's hand after he awakens suggests feelings that go beyond mere gratitude, but she slips away and returns to her room.

The next day, Rochester is gone. He stays away two weeks, and when he does return he brings with him a party of house guests for an extended stay. Among the guests is a Mrs. Ingram and her two daughters, Blanche and Mary. It's obvious that the handsome Blanche is doing her best to snare the affections of Mr. Rochester, but Jane can only suffer her jealousy in silence. One day during the house party, two strange things happen:

1. Mr. Rochester disguises himself as a gypsy woman, and pretending to tell her fortune, tries to find out whether Jane cares for him. She is wary, however, and doesn't reveal her true feelings.
2. Jane is awakened in the middle of the night by calls for help coming from the third floor of the house. The calls are from Mr. Richard Mason, an unexpected visitor who had arrived from Jamaica earlier that day. Mr. Rochester asks Jane to stay with Mr. Mason while he rides to town for the doctor. Jane observes in horror that Mason is

bleeding heavily from stab and bite wounds. Judging by his frantic cry—"She sucked my blood!"—he's been attacked by Grace Poole.

Before the house party ends, Jane is called back to Gateshead to the bedside of the dying Mrs. Reed. Mrs. Reed confesses that three years ago the brother of Jane's dead mother had written from Madeira saying that he wanted to adopt Jane and make her his heir. Out of spite, Mrs. Reed wrote back to the uncle, John Eyre, telling him that Jane died of typhus at Lowood School.

Jane returns to Thornfield, where it is expected that Mr. Rochester will soon marry Blanche Ingram. On Midsummer Eve, however, when Rochester tells Jane that he will have to find her another job after his marriage, she breaks down and reveals her love for him. Then he admits that it's she whom he's loved all along and asks her to marry him.

Two nights before the wedding, Jane awakes to find a strange woman standing over her bed—not Grace Poole, but someone far more frightening, with a swollen, blotchy face and wearing a shapeless white shift. The strange woman tears Jane's bridal veil in two and stomps on it. Rochester assures Jane that the stranger must have been Grace Poole and that her hideous appearance was only a nightmare.

It's the day of the wedding. The ceremony has already begun when it is interrupted by two men—Richard Mason and a lawyer from London, Mr. Briggs. Briggs announces that Rochester already has a wife, Bertha Mason, who is already living at Thornfield! Rochester confesses that his wife, hopelessly and violently insane, lives in the locked rooms on the third floor of the house. Mr. Briggs then reveals that he works for Jane's uncle, Mr. John Eyre, who knew the Mason family and was determined to keep his niece from making a bigamous marriage. (Jane had written to tell him she was getting married.)

Rochester tells Jane that he never loved Bertha and only married her at the urging of his father, who wanted his son to have a rich wife. Because the symptoms of Bertha's insanity were concealed from him before the wedding, he feels that the marriage was never morally valid. (Under the laws of England he cannot obtain a divorce.) He asks Jane to run away to France with him and live as his mistress. She refuses.

Early the next morning, Jane flees Thornfield, traveling as far away as she can on the little money she has. Hungry and destitute, she is taken in by two sisters, Diana and Mary Rivers. Their brother, St. John (sĭn'jŭn) Rivers, gets Jane work teaching at a charity school in the parish where he is a clergyman.

Fearful of scandal, Jane has not told her new friends her correct last name. Some months later, when St. John discovers her true identity by accident, he realizes that she is his missing cousin, Miss Eyre! What's more, he tells Jane that her uncle John Eyre has died and left her a fortune of twenty thousand pounds. Jane decides to share the money with St. John, Diana, and Mary, who have been so kind to her and who are the family she has always yearned for.

St. John is a pale, cold man who brags to Jane that he is overcoming the tendencies of his earthly nature in order to prepare himself for a life of missionary service in India. Among the temptations he overcomes is his love for Rosamund Oliver, a beautiful and wealthy girl who wants to marry him. Because he thinks that Jane, plain and used to hardship as she is, would make a better missionary's wife, St. John proposes to her. Jane, after much inner struggle, rejects this offer of a cold, loveless marriage and decides that the time has come for her to find out what has become of Rochester.

But when Jane returns to Thornfield, she discovers that the house has been destroyed in a fire. Mad Bertha, who started the conflagration, leaped to her death from the burning roof of the house and Rochester, who was trying to rescue her, lost his left hand, one eye, and the sight in his remaining eye.

Jane seeks out Rochester at Ferndean, the isolated hunting lodge where he has been living a hermit's life. Reunited, they realize that they are still deeply in love and decide to marry. In the concluding chapter of the story, we learn that Jane and Rochester have been married for ten years and are idyllically happy.

The Characters

MAJOR CHARACTERS

Jane Eyre

In creating the character of Jane Eyre, Charlotte Brontë did something that was very daring at the time: She presented her readers with a heroine who was not beautiful! In the first half of the 19th century, readers took it for granted that the heroines of novels were supposed to be beautiful, just as we assume that a high fashion model will be slender and glamorous. But Jane Eyre is described as small and plain, a rather mousy-looking young woman who will never be transformed into a femme fatale or a romantic beauty and has no interest in trying to become one.

According to Charlotte Brontë's friend and biographer Mrs. Gaskell, even Charlotte's own sister Emily had her doubts about this decision. Who'd want to read about the adventures of an ordinary-looking heroine? What could possibly happen to such a character that would be interesting to anyone?

A few early readers of the novel did react in exactly the way Emily predicted. One famous critic obviously had *Jane Eyre* in mind when he complained that the reader who purchased a novel only to find that its heroine was "an ugly lady" was the "victim" of a fraud. For the most part, however, Charlotte Brontë's gamble was successful. She had guessed correctly that her readers, whatever their own situation, would find it easy to identify with a character who had doubts about her looks and her attractiveness to others. Today we aren't surprised by a novel whose heroine is not only an outsider, but also a young woman who can't count on beauty to make life easier for her. In fact, the "small, plain" heroine of *Jane Eyre* has been copied so often that she has almost become a cliché. We have to keep reminding ourselves that Jane is the original of the character that we meet so often in romance novels.

Jane Eyre's physical appearance wasn't the only feature that made her an unusual heroine in her day. Charlotte Brontë also broke with custom in insisting that a female character could be the emotional equal of a man. Writing in an era when many people seriously doubted that women were capable of strong emotions, Charlotte Brontë created a heroine who was deeply passionate and felt a need for adventure, excitement, and even a desire for work that matters in the larger scale of human accomplishment. For this reason, even though *Jane Eyre* is a love story told from a woman's point of view, it also appeals to many male readers.

Jane's vivid imagination and strong emotions are the basis of her strength as a character, but we're also told that Jane's being "too passionate" is also a fault. How can this be? You'll find different answers to this question: Jane finds it hard to forgive people who treat her unjustly; she's carried away by her love for Mr. Rochester—even to the point of making him her "idol"—before she knows very much about his past or his true character; and even with St. John, whom she doesn't love, Jane is so susceptible to his influence that she almost makes a decision she knows to be wrong for her.

There are always a few readers who feel disappointed when Jane, the rebel, ends up as a conventional wife and mother, totally devoted to her much older husband. You will have to read the story carefully in order to decide for yourself how much Jane's character changes over time. Is the mature woman, Jane

Eyre, still basically the same personality as the child we meet in Chapter 1? Does becoming a wife mean that Jane has given up her emotional independence? Or has she found a new and more meaningful way of expressing herself in her relationship with Mr. Rochester?

Most readers agree that Jane Eyre is a strong, compelling character. There is much more disagreement about the other characters in the novel. How believable are they? Can you accept them as real people in their own right? Or are they two-dimensional figures, who have no life of their own outside of Jane's perceptions of them?

Mr. Edward Rochester

There are two main areas of controversy over the character of Mr. Rochester.

The first argument has to do with his morals. Under English law at the time, a man whose wife became insane could not get a divorce. Mr. Rochester deals with this problem by hiding his mad wife away in the attic and trying to trick Jane into a bigamous marriage. When he is found out, and the wedding canceled at the last minute, he then asks Jane to run away to France with him and live as his mistress.

Some readers are shocked by Rochester's actions. How could Jane ever love such a person? they ask. How could she ever forgive him for deceiving her?

On the other hand, Rochester has his champions. These readers agree with Rochester when he argues that his first marriage was not a "real" marriage at all; it's just a legal technicality that he can't get a divorce. From this point of view, Jane *should* have agreed to go off to France with him. If she had done so, Rochester would never have been horribly wounded in the fire at Thornfield—and, incidentally, there would have been no story!

How you feel about Rochester's action will depend on your views on personal responsibility. Even though Rochester didn't know his wife was insane, was he partly to blame for marrying a woman he hardly knew, just because she had money and the match was favored by his own father? Was Rochester justified in believing he had a right to happiness, even if it meant deceiving the woman he loved?

Another controversy has nothing to do with Mr. Rochester's morals. Good or bad, is he believable? Some readers find Rochester quite realistic. They point out that many writers of Charlotte Brontë's day, men as well as women, would have been tempted to turn Mr. Rochester into a cardboard villain. Instead, Rochester is a man who has human weaknesses, but who is still worthy of love and forgiveness. However, there is another group of readers which does not find this view convincing in the least. One critic, David Cecil, complained that Rochester is "no flesh and blood man," but merely a fantasy lover as seen through the eyes of a naïve and inexperienced young girl.

Here's something that might help you in making up your own mind about him: Mr. Rochester belongs to a definite fictional type—the Byronic hero. This type, based on the work and life of the poet Lord Byron, is a proud, cynical rebel who refuses to submit to the rules of society. A true Byronic hero always labors under some sort of a curse. Often there is a taint of sin or scandal in his past which becomes forgivable only when we understand the true circumstances, which have been hidden from the rest of the world.

Byronic heroes are usually handsome, but like Lord Byron himself, who was lame, they may have a physical handicap that only increases their sex appeal. Also, though outwardly he's a cynic, the Byronic hero is secretly an idealist. His sensitivity can only be revealed, however, when he manages to find a superior woman who can understand his true nature.

As you read the book, or when you're thinking back over it, try to find some of the ways in which Mr. Rochester fits this description. For instance, he tells Jane that his various mistresses were only distractions from his ten-year search for his "ideal of a woman" (Chapter 27). On the other hand, also look for ways in which Charlotte Brontë tried to go against the type. Mr. Rochester is not at all handsome (or, at least, her heroine doesn't think so). And we often see him in very un-Byronic, and even ludicrous situations—falling off his horse, for example (and that's the first time we see him!), or dressing up in a silly gypsy's costume in order to try to find out whether Jane loves him. In the beginning, Rochester is the worldy older man who teases Jane Eyre about her elflike nature. But soon enough, he admits that her influence over him is very real. "You master me," he tells Jane in Chapter 24. And by the end of the story, he has come around to accepting her view of morality and her belief in God.

Charlotte Brontë certainly seems to have intended Mr. Rochester to be a realistic character. In a letter to her publisher, Brontë wrote: "Mr. Rochester has a thoughtful nature and a very feeling heart; he is neither selfish nor self-indulgent . . . [he] errs, when he does err, through rashness and inexperience. . . . He is taught the severe lessons of experience and has the sense to learn wisdom from them. Years improve him. . . . Such, at least, is the character I meant to portray."

You'll have to decide for yourself whether this description fits the character you meet in the pages of *Jane Eyre*.

Mr. Brocklehurst

When *Jane Eyre* was first published, the obvious resemblance of the character of Mr. Brocklehurst to the real Rev. Carus Wilson, whose school Charlotte and her sisters attended, created a sensation. Many of Mr. Wilson's friends and former pupils rushed to his defense, accusing Charlotte Brontë of exaggerating the hardships at the school and unfairly accusing Mr. Wilson of hypocrisy (particularly since, unlike the character of Brocklehurst, Mr. Wilson did not have a wife and daughters who lived in luxury).

Whether or not Charlotte Brontë was fair to Mr. Wilson, it would be hard to argue that Mr. Brockle-hurst is a well-rounded creation. However, it is inter-esting to know that Brontë was being entirely realistic in the scene where Mr. Brocklehurst threatens ten-year-old Jane with hellfire for her childish misbehav-ior. In real life, the Reverend Mr. Wilson not only forbade his pupils to read novels, he expected them to read stories he wrote himself about the horrible things that happen to little boys and girls who disobey. In one typical story, a little boy violates the Sabbath by going ice skating on Sunday. What happens? He promptly falls through a patch of thin ice, drowns, and goes to hell. And in a true account of an eleven-year-old who died while a student at his school, Mr. Wilson wrote that his reaction was one of rejoicing that God had taken one of the best-behaved children in school—"the one for whose salvation we have the best hope"—since her death may "be the means of rousing many of her schoolfellows to seek the Lord while he may still be found."

Helen Burns

Unlike Mr. Brocklehurst, who is a "a harsh man; at once pompous and meddling"—the very picture of a religious hypocrite—Helen Burns is meant to be sympathetic. Not everyone finds her so. For every reader who admires Helen's saintliness and weeps at her death, there will be another who decides that Helen is too good to be true.

Before you jump to the conclusion that the episodes involving Helen are sentimental and unconvincing, you should remember that in those days the death of children was a fairly common fact of life. People in general were much more aware of the possibility that they might die at any time. Not everyone was as gloomy as Mr. Brocklehurst, by any means, but both adults and children talked openly and often about death to a degree we might find almost morbid. We know that Charlotte Brontë had a real-life model for Helen in her own sister Maria, who fell ill at Cowan Bridge school and died a few days after being sent home. And, ironically, at the very time that Charlotte Brontë was writing about Jane Eyre's failure to see the seriousness of Helen's consumption, she was ignoring the early symptoms of the disease in herself, her brother, and her two sisters.

Even knowing this, maybe you still find yourself wondering whether any real child ever talked the way Helen Burns does in the story. The way Helen is described, she is by no means without faults: she has dirty fingernails, breaks the school rules by reading novels in secret, and so on. Yet you may feel, as some readers do, that in the conversations between Jane and Helen about religion, the author has lost touch with her characters and is setting up an artificial debate between two different philosophical viewpoints.

Bertha Mason Rochester

Mr. Rochester's first wife is hardly a full-fledged character at all. We see her only as a ghostly figure, who roams the halls of Thornfield house in the middle of the night, setting fire to her husband's bed and frightening Jane. In this sense, Bertha is nothing more than an unusually realistic and effective horror story monster. Jane actually sees Bertha only twice: once when Bertha invades her bedroom in the middle of the night, and once in Chapter 27 where Bertha is described as follows: "What it was, whether beast or human being, one could not, at first sight, tell: it grovelled, seemingly, on all fours; it snatched and growled like some strange wild animal . . ." In support of the view that Bertha is nothing more than a device for moving the plot along, notice that even Mr. Rochester's description of her earlier life is curiously vague and unsympathetic. Also, once the time comes for Jane and Rochester to be reunited, Bertha conveniently commits suicide in the fire she starts at Thornfield Hall.

In recent years, feminist critics have become more interested in what the person Bertha Mason means in the story of Jane Eyre. In their view, Helen Burns represents the spiritual side of Jane Eyre's nature while Bertha Mason symbolizes her uncontrolled passion. Note that in Chapter 1, when Jane resists John Reed's bullying, he calls her a "bad animal." And in Chapter 2, Jane is locked in the red-room bedroom because her behaviour has been so "passionate."

Bertha Mason has also fascinated modern women novelists. Jean Rhys' *The Wide Sargasso Sea* is an entire novel written about the youth and early marriage of Rochester's mad wife. Another contemporary novel, Doris Lessing's *The Four-Gated City*, while not explicitly based on *Jane Eyre*, concerns a modern housekeeper, romantically involved with her employer, who discovers that his mentally ill wife lives in the basement of the house. You might find it interesting to compare 20th-century views of the mad wife in these novels with the Bertha Mason we meet in *Jane Eyre*.

St. John Rivers

Just as Edward Rochester is the foil and object of Jane Eyre's passion, St. John (sĭn'jŭn) is the character who reflects Jane's sometimes contradictory ideas about duty and spirituality. St. John is constantly described in terms of images of coldness: He is called cold-hearted and frigid. "His reserve was again frozen over, and my frankness was congealed beneath it . . . he continually made little chilling differences between us . . ." Jane says (Chapter 34). At times St. John seems to take a perverse pleasure in torturing himself. He ignores the inner voices that tell him he's made a wrong decision in entering the ministry. Although "wildly" in love with the beautiful, rich Rosamond Oliver, he finds an excuse to reject her. He seems to relish the prospect of dying young in the tropical heat of India. On the other hand, Jane cannot help admiring St. John for his dedication. While she is planning to spend her new fortune in leisure at Moor House, St. John is preparing to renounce everything to go out into the world and do good works.

Notice that St. John is often described in a way that recalls characters we've met earlier in the story. St. John reminds Jane of a "cold, cumbrous column, gloomy and out of place." Mr. Brocklehurst is described as "a black pillar" (Chapter 4). Like Brocklehurst, St. John subscribes to a grim view of religion, which he seeks to impose on others. But is St. John also a hypocrite? Some readers say no. Unlike Brocklehurst, he is prepared to follow the same harsh rules he would prescribe for others. Others disagree. Who but a hypocrite, they say, would try to convince a woman to marry him by telling her that it is the will of God? St. John wants Jane's total devotion, but is willing to give nothing in return.

St. John is also frequently compared to Helen Burns. "Burn" is a Scottish word meaning "stream" or "brook"; St. John's last name is Rivers. According to this interpretation, Helen, a child, is able to submit to God's will directly and simply. St. John, an adult, cannot submit to God's call except through an intense struggle, which destroys a part of himself.

Some readers even see certain likenesses between St. John and Mr. Rochester. Although opposites in temperament, both men do try to trick Jane into marriage—Rochester by hiding the existence of his wife and St. John by convincing Jane that she must marry him for the sake of duty. Both are also described as frequently moody and withdrawn. Are these similarities purposeful? Probably so, although a few readers have suggested that Charlotte Brontë simply did not have a wide repertoire when it came to male characters on account of her own narrow experience with men. (Brontë was so sensitive to this particular criticism that she began her next novel, Shirley, with a scene in which all of the characters are male.)

There is no one correct judgment on St. John. If you are religious, you'll probably admire his struggle to turn himself into an instrument of God's will. If you are interested in psychology, you're probably more likely to conclude that he hasn't really conquered his earthly desires, just rechanneled them in another direction. Jane Eyre's own judgment of St. John swings dramatically from one scene to the next. In rejecting St. John's proposal of marriage she tells him angrily, "You almost hate me. If I were to marry you, you would kill me. You are killing me now." Yet not long after, in a calmer mood, she tells Diana Rivers, "He is a good and great man: but he forgets, pitilessly, the feelings and claims of little people, in pursuing his own large views."

The final paragraphs of the novel present yet a third view of St. John, comparing him favorably to Greatheart, the Christian warrior in *Pilgrim's Progress:* "Firm, faithful, and devoted; full of energy and zeal, and truth, he labours for his race. . . . He may be stern; he may be exacting: he may be ambitious yet; but his is the sternness of Greatheart. . . . His is the exaction of the apostle, who speaks for Christ when he says— 'Whosoever will come after Me, let him deny himself, and take up his cross and follow Me.' "

SOME MINOR CHARACTERS

Miss Maria Temple

The superintendent of Mr. Brocklehurst's school. Miss Temple befriends Jane, yet you may ask yourself whether she does all she can to stand up to Mr. Brocklehurst's stern edicts. She is a sympathetic character but perhaps not a strong one.

The Reed Family

John Reed, the bully who attacks Jane in Chapter 1, grows up to lead an immoral life and commits suicide while still in his twenties. As for the unloving Mrs. Reed and her two unattractive daughters, Eliza and

Georgiana, some readers have noticed that they resemble the wicked stepmother and stepsisters in Cinderella. If so, then it's interesting to see that by Chapter 21, when Jane returns to visit Gateshead, the Reeds have already lost their power to make her miserable. Why? Has falling in love transformed Jane into a Cinderella after the ball? Or is some other change in Jane's character responsible?

Mrs. Fairfax

The housekeeper at Thornfield is a reassuring figure—neat, sensible, and cheerful. Some readers have also noted, however, that Mrs. Fairfax is also a weak link in the plot. Although she runs the mansion and supervises the servants, Mrs. Fairfax is supposedly unaware that Mr. Rochester is keeping his insane wife on the third floor of the house. Do you find this believable? The novel is vague about how much Mrs. Fairfax may have suspected, and you will notice that, after the truth about Bertha Mason is revealed, Mrs. Fairfax drops out of sight. It would be interesting to hear how she might explain her ignorance of the secret of the house, but we never get the chance.

Blanche Ingram

No characterization in *Jane Eyre* has been the target of as much negative criticism as that of Blanche Ingram. Blanche is an elegant young lady from a titled family who flirts outrageously with Mr. Rochester and, for a time, hopes to marry him. You will notice that Blanche is described as being tall, with an excellent figure and a complexion "as dark as a Spaniard." This might sound to you like the description of a beautiful woman, but you will find that Charlotte Brontë, who was as tiny and pale as Jane Eyre herself, rarely has a good word to say about women who are either large or dark-skinned, or both. Blanche sprinkles her conversation with affected French phrases; she makes fun of another houseguest, Mrs. Dent, who knows less than she does about botany; and she pouts openly after Rochester, dressed as a gypsy, leads her to believe that he's not rich after all.

Some readers, including many who read *Jane Eyre* at the time of its publication, have considered Blanche a fair representative of the spoiled, aristocratic belles of her day. Others can't help suspecting that the portrait of Blanche has been distorted by Jane's—and perhaps even the author's own—feelings of jealousy.

Other Elements

SETTING

In the 1840s, when *Jane Eyre* was written, there were very few ways in which an educated woman could earn her own living. Poor girls might go to work as a house servant or in a factory, but the conditions in these jobs were so bad, and their status so low, that no young woman from a "good" family would consider these alternatives except in extreme desperation. That left teaching, usually as a governess with a wealthy family, as just about the only respectable occupation.

Governesses lived with the families they worked for, so they lived in fairly comfortable surroundings. However, their cash wages were very low, so their work gave them no real financial independence. For the most part, they led lonely and unsatisfying lives. Their status was higher than that of the other servants—and too much mixing with the help was frowned on!—yet they weren't accepted as part of the family either. Unless a governess happened to be unusually attractive, her chances of finding a husband were slim. Most marriages at the time were based on family connections or financial considerations, and an educated woman with no dowry had almost no chance of getting married. Since they didn't have much hope of saving money out of their low salaries, all that most governesses could look forward to was a lonely and uncertain old age, dependent on the kindness of the families they had served.

There had been governess-heroines before Jane Eyre, but they were portrayed as plucky and beautiful—an outsider's fantasy of the independent woman. *Jane Eyre* was the first successful look at the reality of the governess's life. It's not really necessary to know much about the 19th century in order to enjoy the story of *Jane Eyre*, but you'll understand some of Jane's actions a little better if you keep in mind that she's a governess. Jane Eyre is a plain-looking young woman who has been in an all-girl school since she was ten years old. She hasn't had any chance to learn about the ways of gentlemen like Mr. Rochester or about the male sex in general. By the standards of the time, Jane is quite bold in talking to Mr. Rochester as an equal. But when she realizes that his interest in her is romantic, she has to assume that it's not marriage he has in mind. This explains why she is very cautious about revealing her feelings for him. Also, although she works for Mr. Rochester for some months, Jane has very little cash of her own. When she goes to visit the Reeds, Rochester gives her extra money for the trip. And when she decides that she must leave Thornfield rather than become his mistress, Jane has only twenty shillings to her name—just enough money to pay her fare for a two-day trip to a distant part of England.

Governesses were working women. But their security and freedom were very precarious. This is why Jane Eyre is powerfully drawn to the possibility of becoming dependent on a man—either through becoming Mr. Rochester's mistress or St. John Rivers' wife. Yet at the same time, she is also afraid, because her decision, once made, will be forever.

THEMES

How can I find someone to love me? And how can I tell whether the person who loves me is worthy of being loved in return? All of us ask ourselves these questions. For Jane Eyre, the heroine of this story, the prospects of finding happiness in love don't seem very good. At the beginning of the novel, Jane is a poor orphan. Her only known relatives, the Reeds, do not want her. She isn't a pretty girl, and perhaps more important, she doesn't have the knack for pleasing people. As a child, Jane is starved for affection. "If others don't love me, I would rather die than live!" she tells Helen, her only true friend. Yet part of her problem in winning the love of others is that she is "too passionate"—that is, angry, rebellious, and prone to retreat into her own richly imaginative inner world for solace.

Even though circumstances are against Jane, she isn't ready to settle for a man's love on any terms that are offered. She's deeply skeptical of organized religion, but she believes in God. She also has a strong sense of pride and self-respect. So she can only be happy with a man if she can reconcile that love with her love of God and her love for herself. That's a tall order! To fill it, Jane must be prepared to struggle, both against external circumstances and with her own failings and weaknesses.

All readers agree that *Jane Eyre* is a love story. However, they often disagree about just what kind of a love story it is. Many readers are impressed by Jane Eyre's insistence on emotional equality with her lover and see a feminist message in the story. They point to the strong feminist views expressed by Jane in Chapter 12, where she says, "Women are supposed to be very calm generally: but women feel just as men feel; they need exercise for their faculties, and a field for their efforts as much as their brothers do . . ." Other readers feel that Jane's search for a way to reconcile her need for love with her search for a way of life acceptable to God is the most important idea in the story. And still others find it hard to take either the

social or religious aspects of the story very seriously.
For them, the elements of mystery, horror, and thrill-
ing emotional extremes make the book a romantic fantasy. A fourth point of view is that *Jane Eyre* is a story
about the problems of growing up as an outsider
without the support of family or a recognized place in
society—a story rather like Dicken's *David Copperfield*,
except that the main character happens to be
female.

In reading *Jane Eyre*, you may find that just one of
these views matches your own reactions to the story.
Or you may find yourself deciding that *Jane Eyre* fits
more than one of these categories. *Jane Eyre* is a very
personal book, and it affects different readers in different ways.

One thing is certain: *Jane Eyre* is a novel that's meant
to be *enjoyed*, not just picked apart to search for hidden
meanings. For well over a century, readers of both
sexes, all ages, and widely different educational back-
grounds have been entertained by the novel's grip-
ping story. An understanding of the themes and literary artistry of the novel can deepen your pleasure.
However, you don't need any special kind of knowledge in order to understand and identify with the story of Jane Eyre's search for love.

STYLE

Many readers think that Charlotte Brontë's writing
style is her greatest weakness. The style of *Jane Eyre* is
highly charged with emotion, almost feverish in its
intensity. You'll find sentence after sentence stuffed
with lush adjectives and sensual images. Sometimes
the words almost seem to have spilled out onto the
page in a headlong, uncontrolled rush of feeling.
From time to time, you may even feel that the author

has lost track of what she means to say. One sentence often mentioned as an example of this occurs in Chapter 15, where we read of Mr. Rochester: "Pain, shame, ire—impatience, disgust, detestation—seemed momentarily to hold a quivering conflict in the large pupil dilating under his ebony eyebrow." If all this is going on in just one of Rochester's eyes, what can possibly be happening to the other?

If you are the sort of person who prefers writers who are always in control of their prose, and who can describe subtle shadings of emotion, you may find that you become impatient with Charlotte Brontë's style. Bronte is often compared negatively with Jane Austen, whose writing is more restrained, allowing for sharp and witty observations of character and social mores.

On the other hand, most readers agree that the prose style of the novel fits very well with the headstrong, emotional character of the narrator, Jane Eyre. Would you find it easy to believe that Jane was a "passionate" person if she told her story in cool, elegant language? Wouldn't you be more skeptical about some of her frightening experiences at Thornfield if they were told that way? It's possible to be critical of some aspects of Charlotte Brontë's writing and still feel that, on the whole, it's her style that draws readers into the conflicts of the story. Because the language is emotionally powerful, we're able to identify with Jane Eyre, instead of simply pronouncing judgments on her personality.

POINT OF VIEW

Jane Eyre is a first-person narrative, related in the voice of the protagonist, or heroine. Jane Eyre is the "I" of the story, the person whose voice we hear as we read, and everything that happens is seen from her point of view. Nowhere in the novel does the author break the flow of the narrator's voice to give us an objective view of her main character. However, she does remind us once in a while that the story is being told by Jane as a mature woman, looking back on events that happened some years earlier. The mature Jane occasionally comments on the younger Jane's reactions to those events, and sometimes she even addresses you, the Reader, directly. You'll also find occasions where her narrative includes long stories told to Jane by other characters (such as Rochester's accounts of his past), conversations that Jane overhears between other characters, and even accounts of Jane's dreams. These not only add variety to the style but give the reader a chance to check up on the truthfulness of the narrator.

It's important to remember that in a first-person narrative like *Jane Eyre* we know only what the main character tells us. You may well suspect as you read that Jane's opinions aren't always entirely objective— another sort of person might see the events of the story and the personalities of the various characters in an entirely different light. This isn't necessarily a weakness in the novel; in fact, it may be one of its strengths.

But you'll truly enjoy *Jane Eyre* only if you feel a basic trust in the narrator. For the novel to be a success for you, you must be able to imagine that, in Jane's shoes, you might well have felt and acted as she did.

FORM AND STRUCTURE

Jane Eyre is the story of one young woman, told in her own voice and in chronological order, as it happened. In this sense, the structure of the novel is very simple. One critic, Robert Bernard Martin, has gone a step farther in analyzing the form of *Jane Eyre*. He compares the novel to a five-act play, divided according to the five different places where Jane lives during the course of her life—the Reeds' house, Gateshead; Lowood school; Thornfield; Moor House; and Ferndean. Each time Jane journeys to a new locale she's ready to begin another stage in her emotional life, and her journeys are described in a way that builds the reader's suspense.

On another level, however, the plot of *Jane Eyre* is very complicated. Suspense plays a large role in the story. In chapter after chapter, Jane finds an answer to one question that has been bothering her only to be confronted with yet another mystery or dilemma. In the end, some of these questions are resolved through melodramatic and highly improbable coincidences. Many of these coincidences are set in motion by Jane's long-lost uncle, John Eyre—a character we're never told about in the beginning of the story, and who never actually appears in person. Some readers feel that an author who constructs a plot in this way is not quite playing fair with them; they feel cheated. Other readers don't mind at all. And a third group argues that since *Jane Eyre* is a novel that deals with horror, the supernatural, and the secrets of the human heart, we shouldn't hold the plot to the same standard of probability we might demand in a more realistic story. You'll have to decide for yourself which view you agree with.

The Story

CHAPTER 1

As the novel opens, Mrs. Reed, a well-to-do widow, is sitting by the fireplace in her comfortable living room. Around her are her three children—Eliza, Georgiana, and fourteen-year-old John. A fat, spoiled bully, John is still his mother's favorite. She stuffs him with rich food and keeps him out of school because she's convinced that he is too "delicate" to keep up with his schoolwork.

Off to one side of the room is Jane Eyre, a ten-year-old orphan who lives with the Reed family. We can see right away what Jane's life must be like—we learn that she's being punished for the crime of not being cheerful enough. Jane is an unloved, unwanted child, an outsider in the only home she has ever known.

Jane wanders off to the next room and settles herself on a small window seat. Hidden from view behind the scarlet curtains that decorate the window, Jane can read in peace. Her book, Bewick's *History of British Birds*, is filled with romantic illustrations of the Far North—Norway, Siberia, the Arctic—and Jane's lively imagination soon carries her away into her own fantasy world.

But she doesn't get to enjoy her book for long. John Reed finds Jane in her hiding place and demands that she give him the book. At fourteen, he is already a tyrant. He reminds Jane that he is the young master of the house and that everything in it, including the books, all belong to him—or will in a few years. Jane, he says, is nothing but a penniless dependent who ought to be out on the streets begging instead of living in comfort "with gentleman's children like us." With that, he picks up the heavy book and throws it. She falls against the door and cuts her head.

Jane has always been too afraid of John to stand up to him. This time, however, she is furious. "You are like the Roman emperors!" she shouts, thinking of tyrants, such as Nero and Caligula, whom she has read about. Jane's willingness to defend herself makes John lose all self-control. He flies at her and starts pulling her hair. She feels a drop of blood trickling down her neck, and it gives her the courage to fight back.

Just as Jane starts hitting John, Mrs. Reed rushes in, and of course she jumps to the conclusion that Jane started the fight. She orders her to be locked up in an empty bedroom as punishment. As Jane is being dragged out of the room by the nursemaid, Bessie, and Mrs. Reed's maid, Miss Abbot, she hears one of them say disapprovingly, "Did you ever see such a picture of passion!"

NOTE: By this time—if you're like most readers—you're already very much on Jane's side. Weren't there times in your own childhood when other children picked on you—and you ended up taking the blame? Is there anything more infuriating? On the other hand, you're a few years older—maybe you can see things differently now. If you have younger brothers or sisters, you can see that children's fights are hardly ever completely one-sided.

But as you read the first few chapters of *Jane Eyre*, notice how quickly they pull us into a child's view of the world. The narrator—Jane—is supposed to be looking back on something that happened to her years ago, but she's just as angry as ever. And she makes us angry too. She doesn't bother to wonder how the incident must have looked from Mrs. Reed's point of view, or to ask whether John was really as bad as he seemed. Some readers feel that this is the best thing about Jane Eyre—it brings us back to the strong emotions we felt as children. But others say that the job of the author is to give us a new perspective on things, not just to reinforce a one-sided—and in this case, childish—view of why people behave the way they do.

As you read on, remember that phrase "picture of passion" (it's an old-fashioned way of describing a temper tantrum). In future chapters we're going to hear more, both good and bad, about Jane's "passionate" nature.

CHAPTER 2

Kicking and screaming, Jane is hauled upstairs by Bessie and Miss Abbot. They're both shocked by her behavior, but their reactions aren't quite the same. Miss Abbot reminds Jane coldly that she's "less than a servant," since she does nothing to earn her keep in the house. And she even threatens that if Jane doesn't behave "something bad might come down the chimney and fetch you away." Bessie is more sympathetic. She urges Jane to behave better in the future, but for her own good, so that Mrs. Reed won't send Jane away to the poorhouse.

As punishment, Jane is locked up in the red-room—an unused bedroom furnished with dark red drapes, a red carpet, and heavy mahogany furniture. The history of the room is even gloomier than its furniture. It was here, nine years earlier, that Mr. Reed died and his body was laid out until the day of the funeral.

NOTE: Funeral homes weren't used in Victorian times. The dead were kept at home, sometimes for several days.

At first, thinking about Mr. Reed makes Jane feel better. Mr. Reed was her uncle, her dead mother's brother, and Jane feels sure that if he were still alive he'd treat her better than his widow does. She's heard that Mr. Reed, on his deathbed, made his wife promise to treat Jane as one of the family, and she imagines how angry his spirit would be if it came back to earth and saw that Mrs. Reed is disobeying his dying wish.

By now it is twilight, the rain is beating on the window, the wind is howling. The room is dark and cold. Little by little, the thought of Mr. Reed's ghost no longer seems so comforting. What if it really did come back?

Suddenly, a beam of light shines through the room. Jane's heart beats faster. She hears a strange sound, like the "rushing of wings." She screams in terror.

Jane gets no sympathy from Mrs. Reed. She and Miss Abbot agree that Jane is only pretending to be frightened so they'll let her out of the room. Her story about seeing a ghost is just another lie—even worse than the lie she told about John Reed hitting her first. Mrs. Reed locks Jane up inside the room again and Jane immediately faints dead away.

NOTE: Was Mr. Reed's ghost really in the room? In narrating this episode, the adult Jane Eyre looks back on this frightening moment in her own childhood and decides that there must have been a rational explanation for everything. For example, the beam of light was probably caused by someone carrying a lantern across the lawn outside the window. But, like so many readers, you may still feel that young Jane's fear was real—and a lot more convincing than any attempt to explain it.

As you read on, you'll find that *Jane Eyre* often reads like a horror story. Weird and uncanny things are always happening to Jane. Charlotte Brontë doesn't ask us to believe literally in ghosts. But she does manage to keep us guessing. How much of what happens to Jane is real, and how much is the product of her overactive imagination?

Haunted house stories, called Gothics, were very popular at the time *Jane Eyre* was written. The most famous of these, Mary Shelley's *Frankenstein*, is still read today. Like the authors of these books, Charlotte Brontë uses the supernatural to generate suspense and keep us turning the pages to find out what will happen next. But *Jane Eyre* goes a step beyond the horror story. By mixing real life and the supernatural, it keeps asking questions: Where do you find the line between the "real" and the "unreal"? Is there such a thing as a ghost? What about omens? What about telepathy? Or dreams that foretell the future? During the course of her story, Jane herself makes up her mind about some of these things. You don't necessarily have to agree with her answers, but see if you think they make sense for *her*.

CHAPTER 3

When Jane comes to, she is in the nursery with Bessie and Mr. Lloyd, an apothecary.

NOTE:　　In Victorian times, apothecaries, or pharmacists, sometimes made house calls. We're told that Mrs. Reed calls a medical doctor when she or her own children are sick, but lets the apothecary treat Jane and the servants. What does this say about Mrs. Reed?

Jane's fright in the red-room has left her so nervous that she can't sleep or eat. Bessie does her best to comfort Jane, but you may wonder whether she might be doing more harm than good. For example, Bessie has heard other stories about Mr. Reed's ghost and half believes that Jane really did see a spirit. Even though the story never says so, we can't help wondering whether Bessie's ghost stories are partly responsible for putting these ideas into Jane's head. Bessie also tries to amuse Jane by giving her a copy of *Gulliver's Travels*. If you know anything about this book—about a man who travels to lands populated by giants and tiny people and other strange beings—you have to wonder whether it is quite the thing to calm Jane down after her frightening experience.

Mr. Lloyd returns the next day. He sees how unhappy Jane is with the Reeds and wants to help her. But when he suggests that Jane might be better off going to live with some poor relatives, she is horrified. All Jane knows about poverty is what she's learned from the Reeds—a stereotype of the poor as cruel and degraded, hardly better than animals. As bad as things are where she is, she is not heroic enough to want to exchange her situation for a life of poverty.

Mr. Lloyd has another suggestion—that Jane might like to go away to school. Jane's notions of what boarding school would be like are vague, but she imagines it's a place where young ladies are taught to paint lovely landscapes and read books in French. She tells Mr. Lloyd that she would indeed like to be sent to school.

Jane has never been told anything about her parents. Now, late one night, she overhears Bessie and Miss Abbot talking and learns for the first time that her mother, the rich Miss Reed, defied her family by marrying a poor minister, Mr. Eyre. Now more than ever Jane feels a horror of poverty! Her own mother was never forgiven for the crime of marrying a poor man. And Jane is still paying the price of the Reeds' disapproval.

NOTE: Many children fantasize sometimes that they're orphans. If you're angry with your parents, it can be comforting to think that they are not your real mother and father. Maybe one of the reasons for *Jane Eyre*'s popularity over the years is that the story brings such common fantasies vividly to life. Think back over the first three chapters and see if there other things that not only remind you of experiences in your own childhood but actually make you feel the emotions you felt at the time. Remember, from Chapter 1, the blind rage Jane feels at being blamed for her fight with John Reed, when it was *he* who threw a book at her? That's one example. Can you find some others?

CHAPTER 4

One day, about three months after Mr. Lloyd's visit, Mrs. Reed calls Jane into the breakfast room for an interview with a stranger. This turns out to be Mr. Brocklehurst—a tall, thin man dressed in black from head to toe. Mr. Brocklehurst addresses Jane by bending over so that his face is just a few inches away from hers and asking "Do you know where the wicked go when they die?"

"What a face . . . !" thinks Jane, "what a great nose! and what a mouth! and what large prominent teeth!"

NOTE: Does this description remind you of someone? What about the wolf in "Little Red Riding Hood?" It is worth rereading this scene just to see how the author suggests this comparison without ever so much as mentioning the word wolf. When Jane first sets eyes on Mr. Brocklehurst, he is so tall he looks to her like a "black pillar." He is described as "sable-clad," which means dressed in black, although of course sable is also a kind of fur, which is dark brown or black. Later, Jane notices other telling details, including Brocklehurst's bushy eyebrows and his unusually large feet.

Even though she's taken aback by Mr. Brocklehurst's morbid questions, Jane doesn't let him get the best of her. When he asks her how she can avoid going to hell, Jane refuses to give him the answer that she knows he wants. Instead, she replies, "I must keep in good health and not die."

NOTE: We can't help silently cheering Jane on for having the courage to talk back to the awful Mr. Brocklehurst. Even so (and especially if you happen to be religious), you may not feel quite satisfied with Jane's answer. No matter how healthy we may be, we still have to face death someday. What then? Jane is soon going to learn that rebellion and a quick wit won't help her to avoid some of life's grimmer tragedies. Later on she'll have to think beyond her hasty answer to Mr. Brocklehurst's question.

Mrs. Reed tells Brocklehurst that Jane is a deceitful child, and he promises that his school, Lowood, will be just the place to make Jane repent her bad habits. Stung at hearing herself called a liar, Jane waits until Mr. Brocklehurst has gone and then lashes out at Mrs. Reed. "I will never call you aunt again as long as I live," she cries. "I will never come to see you when I am grown up. . . . People think you are a good woman, but you are bad; hard-hearted. *You* are deceitful!"

This outburst leaves Jane feeling a sense of triumph. But not for long. Jane wants to be loved, but then she has to admit that she is not very lovable. She can't change the fact that she's plain and awkward, but she does think often about changing her behavior. She's sure that her worst fault is that she is "too passionate"—that is, she has strong emotions and isn't good at disguising them to make herself more acceptable. Only Bessie disagrees with this view; the kind servantwoman loves Jane enough to see the loneliness that underlies Jane's rebellion. She warns Jane not to be afraid to reach out and show affection. Jane responds by giving Bessie a warm good-bye kiss.

CHAPTER 5

Jane's first day at Lowood School confirms her worst expectations. All of the girl students, who range in age from nine to twenty years old, have to wear ugly brown dresses covered by pinafores. In the morning they wash in basins of ice cold water. All day long they're marched from place to place, moving from meals to prayers to classes to the sound of clanging bells and the voices of teachers commanding, "Silence!" The food is terrible. For supper on Jane's first night, the girls have only a thin oat cake with water to drink. At breakfast the next morning, the porridge is so badly burned that Jane, although terribly hungry, cannot bring herself to eat.

Miss Temple, who runs the school for Mr. Brocklehurst, isn't a bad person—in fact, she does what she can. When noon comes, for example, Miss Temple tries to make up for the awful breakfast by ordering a special treat of bread and cheese for the girls. However, she doesn't have either the authority or the courage to force Mr. Brocklehurst to hire a better cook. How you judge Miss Temple will depend on whether or not you think it is right for a person to work within a bad system in the hope of mitigating its evils. Is Miss Temple helping the girls at Lowood by making their lives a little easier than they might otherwise be? Or does Miss Temple only make matters worse by staying at her job and keeping Mr. Brocklehurst's system running smoothly?

NOTE: There's room for more than one verdict on Miss Temple's character. But what about the kind of "charity" practiced at Lowood school? Mr. Brocklehurst doesn't believe in coddling the poor. In his opinion, the sooner the girls learn to put up with hardship, the more self-reliant they will be in later life. Today we still hear this point of view (maybe not quite as extreme) every time the subject of poverty comes up: Giving the poor too much only makes them dependent on handouts. There's no doubt what Charlotte Brontë thought about this attitude. She stacks the deck against Mr. Brocklehust by making him as nasty and hypocritical as possible.

We know what kind of charity the author is against. But what kind is she for? Is she arguing in favor of social equality? Or is she only condemning Mr. Brocklehurst's self-righteous attitude?

There are always a few readers who suspect the author herself of being a bit hypocritical about poverty. We're supposed to feel very sorry for the "nice girls" at Lowood. But what about poor people who don't happen to come from "nice" middle-class families? Later in the book (Chapter 31) we'll see that Jane herself is a little snobbish about her lower-class pupils. You'll have to decide for yourself whether the attitude toward charity in *Jane Eyre* is always consistent.

CHAPTER 6

Jane's first friend at Lowood is an older girl named Helen Burns. Helen loves reading, but the school's nastiest teacher, Miss Scatcherd, constantly picks on her because she's dreamy and a little clumsy. Jane can't understand why Helen submits to Miss Scatcherd's persecutions without complaining. Helen quotes the New Testament: "Love your enemies; bless them that curse you; do good to them that hate you and despitefully use you."

Jane argues that this attitude only encourages people like Miss Scatcherd who enjoy picking on the weak. "When we are struck at without a reason," Jane argues, "we should strike back again very hard; I am sure we should—so hard as to teach the person who struck us never to do it again."

NOTE: ˚ Submission or resistance? Pacifism or self-defense? Which is the best way to respond to evil?

Even Jane, the rebel, doesn't mean to say that she'd actually hit a teacher. She just means that she'd find some way to fight back against unfair treatment. Many readers feel that Jane is right and that Helen is simply too good to be believable. A few even get angry at Helen; they argue that people who submit to evil are cooperating with it. Another view, probably closer to Charlotte Brontë's own, is that Jane and Helen represent opposite extremes, with neither being completely correct. Jane wants to fight every battle and is in danger of becoming a bitter person. Helen is moral, almost saintly, but perhaps not very well prepared to survive in an imperfect world.

CHAPTER 7

After an absence of several months, Mr. Brocklehurst pays a visit to the school. He begins by lecturing Miss Temple for giving the girls extra meals of bread and cheese. Then he notices a girl who has naturally curly red hair, and he orders that the barber come to cut it off the very next day. Even natural curls are forbidden at Lowood School!

Mr. Brocklehurst's speech is interrupted by the arrival of his wife and two daughters. They're wearing silk and velvet, and the girls have fancy beaver fur hats with ostrich plumes. Their hairdos are elaborately curled, and Mrs. Brocklehurst is even wearing a fashionably curly hairpiece!

Not at all bothered by this evidence of his hypocrisy, Brocklehurst goes on to single out Jane Eyre, announcing to the whole school Mrs. Reed's charge that she is a liar. Brocklehurst warns the other girls that Jane is such a bad influence that they should not talk to her all day, and he sentences her to stand for half an hour on the punishment stool in the center of the room. Jane is on the point of bursting into tears, but Helen Burns finds an excuse to pass by where Jane is standing and flashes her a smile of encouragement. Helen may believe in obedience, but she is a loyal friend above all.

CHAPTER 8

In spite of having Helen on her side, Jane can't get over her humiliation at being singled out as a liar in front of the whole school. Helen tells her that no one will believe Mr. Brocklehurst, and that Jane shouldn't worry too much about what others think about her: The important thing is that Jane's conscience is clear. Jane disagrees. "If others don't love me, I would rather die than live," she tells Helen.

Once again the two girls have a disagreement about values: Which matters more—what other people think of you, or how you feel about yourself?

Miss Temple comes looking for Jane and invites both girls to come to her room. As Helen predicted, Miss Temple finds it hard to believe Mr. Brocklehurst's charges. More calmly than usual, Jane tells her the true story of her life with the Reeds and begs Miss Temple to write to Mr. Lloyd, the apothecary, who can confirm that Jane was never a bad girl, just miserable and unwanted. Miss Temple agrees.

Then she invites Jane and Helen to share her tea and buttered toast. The portions are tiny—even Miss Temple doesn't rate high enough with the cook to get second helpings—but she brings out a cake of her own. Two hungry girls are in heaven.

NOTE: In writing this scene, Charlotte Brontë must have been thinking about her own days at Cowan Bridge school where the pupils were served dry bread six days a week, with "a scraping of butter" on Sundays. In a place where neither the students nor the teachers ever get quite enough to eat, Miss Temple's invitation to tea is more than a casual gesture. At last someone in authority is giving Jane the approval she craves.

A week later Jane's triumph is complete when Miss Temple announces to the entire school that Mr. Lloyd has answered her letter. He takes Jane's side, and she's cleared of the charge of lying.

CHAPTER 9

Jane has begun to settle down at Lowood and is working hard at her studies. But in late spring, the school routine is interrupted by tragedy. Forty-five of Lowood's 80 pupils fall ill with typhus. Ironically enough, the epidemic makes life easier for the girls who are still healthy. The teachers are so busy tending the sick that there's plenty of free time, and since so many girls aren't eating their regular meals, there's enough food to go around. Jane isn't even particularly worried about the absence of her friend Helen. She's been told that Helen has consumption; Jane thinks this is a mild disease and assumes that Helen is in no immediate danger.

NOTE: Consumption is what's now called tuberculosis, and it was very common in Charlotte Brontë's day. It could be a long and slow disease, but many of its victims were very young people—remember, that's what all the Brontë children died of. Today tuberculosis is fairly rare and can be treated, but there was no cure for it then.

One day Jane sees the doctor leaving, and the nurse tells her that Helen "will not be here long." Suddenly Jane understands. The nurse doesn't mean that Helen is being sent home. Helen is dying!

Jane is told she can't see Helen, but she sneaks into her room while the nurse is asleep. Helen comforts her friend by telling her that she doesn't mind the prospect of death. "I have faith: I am going to God," she says.

Jane is skeptical. How can Helen be so sure of God's love when he sends so much suffering her way? "Where is God?" she cries. "What is God?"

But Helen's faith can't be shaken. The girls fall asleep in each other's arms, and when Jane wakes up Helen is—dead.

CHAPTER 10

It's now eight years later. As she looks back on this period of her life, Jane recalls that the typhus epidemic led to many changes for the better at Lowood. The wealthy citizens of the district decided to investigate conditions at the school and, as a result, Mr. Brocklehurst's power was reduced and many of his harsh rules were eliminated or reformed.

Jane became one of the school's best pupils, and she's remained on the staff as a teacher for the two years since her graduation. The unexpected marriage of Miss Temple, who has been Jane's good friend and mentor, starts Jane thinking that perhaps the time has come for her to leave Lowood and see something more of the world. She advertises in the newspaper for a job as a governess and receives one offer of work—from a Mrs. Fairfax at Thornfield. She decides to accept.

Just before Jane leaves to take up her new job, she receives a surprise visit from Bessie. The Reeds' servant, now happily married, is very impressed by the way Jane has turned out. "You are quite a lady!" she exclaims when she learns that Jane can read French and paint watercolors. Bessie tells Jane that seven years earlier a Mr. Eyre, the brother of Jane's father, came looking for her at Gateshead. He didn't come to see Jane at Lowood because he was sailing for the island of Madeira in two days and didn't have time to make the trip to the school. But don't forget him; we'll hear more from this mysterious relative later in the story.

CHAPTER 11

By the time Jane arrives at Thornfield, the house where she is to work as governess, she is trembling with nervousness. What if Mrs. Fairfax turns out to be another Mrs. Reed?

Much to her relief, however, she finds that Mrs. Fairfax is an elderly lady, plainly but neatly dressed. She welcomes Jane kindly by ordering a plate of sandwiches from the kitchen. Jane is very surprised, and she's so naive about the ways of the wealthy that she doesn't realize until the next day that Mrs. Fairfax is not the lady of the house at all; she's the housekeeper.

Jane's first impression of Thornfield is reassuring. But there are a few hints of mystery: Mr. Rochester, Thornfield's owner and Jane's employer, isn't there, and Mrs. Fairfax explains vaguely that he's a "rather peculiar" man who spends much of his time traveling.

Jane's only pupil is a little French girl, Adèle Varens. She's outgoing and friendly and entertains her new governess by singing an operatic song about a woman who has been abandoned by her lover—a subject the prim Jane thinks is "in bad taste" for a performance by a child of ten. Adèle is Mr. Rochester's ward, but Mrs. Fairfax has no idea who the girl's parents are or how she came into Mr. Rochester's care—another mystery!

Finally, Mrs. Fairfax takes Jane on a tour of Thornfield Hall. She even takes her up to the roof to show off the view from the battlements (ornamental balconies). On their way down, Jane notices that certain rooms on the third floor are shut off from the rest of the house. From behind one of the closed doors she hears a loud, low-pitched laugh—one that sounds more tragic than humorous. Mrs. Fairfax tells her it's most likely one of the servants, a woman named Grace Poole, who often uses those rooms for sewing.

NOTE: Jane goes out of her way to tell us she didn't think the laughter was ghostly or supernatural. Does she convince you? Maybe Brontë assures us that Jane is a sensible person, not easily frightened, in order to make us wonder whether there *is* something supernatural about the laughter? This episode may remind you of a scene in a horror movie where the hero or heroine is unknowingly walking into a dangerous situation, but *we* know that there's a monster lurking around the corner, waiting to pounce. In this novel, however, the author has more than one extra twist up her sleeve. For instance, Jane thought she saw a ghost back in Chapter 2, so maybe she's not quite as reasonable as she claims to be. And of course the laughter hasn't come from a ghost. Everything in this story turns out to be more complicated than we at first expect.

CHAPTER 12

Several months go by. Jane is satisfied with her work, but she finds the quiet life at Thornfield rather boring. In her spare time, she often goes up to the roof to walk along the battlements and daydream. Her everyday life may be dull, but her imagination is constantly churning with dreams of adventure in faraway places. "It is vain to say that human beings ought to be satisfied with tranquillity," Jane tells us, "they must have action; and they will make it if they cannot find it."

Sometimes she paces the corridor on the third floor, where she often hears the eerie laughter that frightened her the first time she came to this part of the house. She finds it hard to believe these sounds come from Grace Poole, who's untalkative but quite respectable-looking woman whenever Jane sees her in the halls.

One wintry afternoon, Jane is on her way to the post office when she stops on the hill above Thornfield to watch the sunset. This peaceful scene is soon interrupted by the sound of hoofbeats. However, the first creature to appear out of the woods is not a horse but a huge black-and-white dog with a head like a lion's. It crosses Jane's mind that perhaps she is seeing a Gytrash—a supernatural being that attacks travelers after dark.

This scare lasts only a few seconds. Then a man on horseback comes into view. The horse slips on the icy road, the rider is thrown to the ground, and Jane rushes to help him. The stranger isn't badly hurt, and he refuses Jane's offer to go for help. He asks who Thornfield belongs to and seems quite puzzled when Jane admits that although she is the governess there she has never seen the owner, Mr. Rochester. The stranger then asks Jane to fetch his horse, which is grazing nearby; but Jane, unused to horses, is afraid to get hear the spirited-looking animal. Instead, she helps the rider to limp to the horse's side and get mounted again, and she goes on to mail her letter.

It's not until later that evening, when Jane sees the same black-and-white dog sitting happily in front of the fire at Thornfield, that she finds out the stranger was none other than Mr. Rochester himself!

This first encounter with Mr. Rochester seems to justify Mrs. Fairfax's description of him as peculiar. Why doesn't he introduce himself to Jane right away? Is he just being playful? Is he feeling embarrassed at meeting one of his own employees under such awkward circumstances? Or is it a little bit cruel of him to tease a shy, unsophisticated governess in this way? Most readers, like Jane herself, find the brooding, unconventional Mr. Rochester very attractive. For a few, however, he remains unconvincing, a two-dimensional character, and even unpleasant.

NOTE: In this very personal story, even the weather echoes Jane's moods. The icy cold, moonlit night creates an aura of suspense surrounding Jane's first impression of Mr. Rochester. Also, just before dark, Jane was watching a brilliant crimson sunset—many readers have noticed that the color crimson, or red, seems to be associated with strong, passionate feelings throughout the novel. Can you remember other examples in the chapters you've already read? For instance, look back at the very beginning of the book. And as you read on, keep looking—you'll find lots of places where Brontë uses the weather or nature to create mood.

CHAPTER 13

Jane does not see Mr. Rochester again until the next evening, after dinner. At this time, Rochester tells her then when he first saw her sitting near the road the previous evening he thought of "fairy tales" and wondered if she had bewitched his horse. Jane doesn't mention that she was having similar thoughts about him, but Rochester's confession makes her feel that there's some special bond between the two of them. Normally, Jane is shy with strangers, but soon she and her employer are engaged in a light-hearted conversation about the "men in green" (fairies), much to the confusion of Mrs. Fairfax.

Rochester asks to see Jane's watercolors. He agrees with her judgment that she isn't yet a very skillful painter, but he says there is thought in them and insists the thoughts are "elfish." "And who taught you to paint wind?" he asks, amazed. Then, for no reason that Jane can see, his mood abruptly turns gloomy and Jane and Mrs. Fairfax are dismissed from the room.

After a cheerful beginning the chapter ends on a note of mystery. Mrs. Fairfax explains to Jane that Edward Rochester, their employer, didn't get along with his father and elder brother, which is why he has spent so much of his life traveling in Europe. Furthermore, Mr. Rochester never expected to be the owner of Thornfield; he inherited the house just nine years ago after his brother died without a will. Mrs. Fairfax hints that unpleasant memories of his brother keep Mr. Rochester from spending more time at home.

CHAPTER 14

For the next few days Mr. Rochester is occupied with business and his gentlemen friends from the neighborhood, and Jane and Adèle hardly see him. Finally, one evening after dinner he sends for them in the drawing room and gives Adèle a beautifully wrapped box containing a rose-colored silk dress—

the present from France she has been eagerly hoping for.

Noticing Jane looking at him, Mr. Rochester suddenly asks her whether she thinks he's handsome. Jane, all too honestly, blurts out, "No, sir." She doesn't believe in flattery.

He keeps questioning her, and she begins to suspect that he's amusing himself at her expense. She refuses to be drawn into the game. But he's not offended; he admires her proud, outspoken manner. When Jane says that no one "free-born" would stand for being insulted, even by an employer, Mr. Rochester answers cynically, "Most things free-born will submit to anything for a salary." But Jane is the exception. "I find it impossible to be conventional with you," Rochester confesses.

Adèle comes into the room to show off her new dress, and falls to one knee in front of Mr. Rochester, saying in French that she is thanking him "as her mother would have done." Rochester winces at this and tells Jane that, even though he doesn't love Adèle, he's bringing her up in order to pay for numerous sins. Once again, just when Jane is beginning to feel comfortable in Mr. Rochester's company, she gets a hint that there's some dark, and perhaps guilty, secret connected with his past.

CHAPTER 15

Rochester keeps his promise not to "be conventional" with Jane. One day, as they walk together on the grounds of the mansion, he confesses that Céline Varens, Adèle's mother, was his mistress. The love affair ended on a sour note when Rochester went to visit Céline unexpectedly one night and overheard her making fun of him in a conversation with a French officer. Céline, who had been a dancer with the French opera, later ran off to Italy with still another lover, abandoning Adèle. He tells Jane he doesn't believe that Adèle is his child but has decided to take responsibility for seeing that she grows up away from the "slime and mud" of Paris in a wholesome English atmosphere.

NOTE: For many young Englishmen, a trip to Paris meant their first chance to live away from the watchful eyes of their families—hence, the English view of Paris as a very immoral place.

Even while Mr. Rochester is making this frank confession, there are hints that he's not telling Jane everything. At one point he interrupts his story to glare darkly in the direction of Thornfield's battlements. He tells Jane that he has seen a vision of his destiny taunting him: "You like Thornfield? Like it if you can! Like it if you dare!"

Not long after, Jane is wakened in the middle of the night by a "demoniac laugh"—this time coming from right outside her bedroom. When she opens her door, she smells something burning. Someone has set fire to the heavy curtains around Mr. Rochester's bed. Jane tries to wake him, but the smoke has made him groggy. She douses the flames with a pitcher of water, which rouses him. When she tells him about hearing Grace Poole's laugh in the hall, he agrees—not very convincingly—that it must have been Grace who set the fire. Rochester makes Jane promise not to mention the incident to anyone.

When Jane starts to go back to her room, Rochester hints in a roundabout way that she might like to stay and comfort him. She ignores the suggestion, but secretly she is thrilled by this evidence of Rochester's interest in her. She is already well on her way to falling in love.

NOTE: Manners and morals have changed so much since the 19th century that it's possible you won't realize how daring this last scene actually is. For a governess to be in her employer's bedroom in the middle of the night was rather risqué, no matter how good a reason there might be for it. Even more than most women, governesses had to be very careful of their reputations. A hint of scandal, even if there was no basis for it, could make it impossible to find work. What wife would hire a governess who might be tempted to carry on with her husband or a grown son? This is one reason why Jane is very careful not to let anyone, even Rochester himself, know how she really feels about him.

CHAPTER 16

The next morning, Jane is on her way downstairs when she notices the servant girl, Leah, is busy cleaning up the mess in Mr. Rochester's room. Grace Poole is with her. Jane tries to question Grace about the fire, but soon has the uncomfortable feeling that Grace is also trying to find out how much Jane knows. Among other things, Grace asks Jane whether she keeps her bedroom door bolted at night. Jane has never done this, but she decides that from now on she will.

Why is Grace Poole at Thornfield? Grace is hardly ever seen downstairs in the house and spends almost all her time alone in the locked room on the third floor. Jane guesses that Grace is about the same age as Mr. Rochester (in her late thirties) and wonders whether there was some past connection between her and the master, perhaps a love affair. It seems to Jane that Grace has some sort of power over Mr. Rochester. On the other hand, she finds it hard to imagine a romance between this stolid, unsmiling woman and Rochester, even one that might have happened many years ago.

Downstairs, Jane learns from Mrs. Fairfax that Mr. Rochester has gone away to attend a house party at one of the other great houses in the district. Mrs. Fairfax mentions that among the guests will be Miss Blanche Ingram, a raven-haired beauty of twenty-five, who was the "belle of the evening" at a party given at Thornfield six years ago. She and Mr. Rochester sang a duet together. This casual conversation throws Jane into a turmoil of jealousy. Mrs. Fairfax denies that Mr. Rochester has any plans to marry Blanche, but Jane decides she had better prepare herself for the worst. Back in her room, Jane sketches a picture of herself as Mr. Rochester must see her: a plain, poor governess. Then she forces herself to paint a delicate portrait of the lovely Miss Ingram, based on Mrs. Fairfax's description.

CHAPTER 17

Ten days later, Mr. Rochester sends word that he'll soon be returning home and bringing the house party guests with him. Suddenly, gloomy Thornfield comes alive with activity.

On the second night after the guests arrive, Mr. Rochester orders Adèle and Jane to join his company in the drawing room after dinner. Little Adèle is delighted at the prospect of being part of a grown-up party. However, the invitation only makes Jane more miserable. She has nothing to wear except a pearl gray silk dress which she purchased for Miss Temple's wedding. Jane isn't much interested in clothes, but she is human enough to hate the thought of how frumpy she will look in comparison to the other elegantly gowned ladies.

The evening turns out to be just as bad as Jane had feared. The other women are dressed in the height of fashion, reminding Jane of "a flock of white plumy birds." Blanche Ingram flirts outrageously with Mr. Rochester. And worst of all, Blanche and her mother—ignoring Jane's presence—get involved in a lengthy conversation about how "ridiculous" governesses are, making fun of the faults of various ones who have worked for their family. As if this weren't enough, Blanche launches into a speech on the relative importance of beauty in men and women, concluding confidently that "an ugly *woman* is a blot on the face of creation."

NOTE: Some readers feel that the house party episode is the weakest part of the novel. They complain that Charlotte Brontë didn't know how upper class people really behaved and that her dialogue for their conversations—which are loaded with the affected use of foreign phrases and cloying endearments such as "lily-flower"—is crude and inaccurate. Other readers find that the author has done a good job of showing the contrast between Jane and the rich people, reminding us exactly what it feels like to be the butt of rude and condescending remarks.

CHAPTER 18

Jane's spirits reach their low point when one evening, during a game of charades, Mr. Rochester and Blanche Ingram appear dressed up as a bride and groom. Jane reflects that she doesn't believe Mr. Rochester truly loves Blanche. She can see that

Blanche, despite her fine figure and outgoing personality, is cold-hearted and not very bright. Surely Mr. Rochester sees this, too. If he marries Blanche, it will only be for her money and position in society!

NOTE: Does Jane's reasoning sound convincing to you? It's nice to think that we fall in love because we are attracted by our beloved's inner goodness. But truthfully, aren't most of us influenced by appearances? The story goes on to suggest that Jane is right in thinking that Rochester could never love a woman like Blanche. Still, some readers suspect that Jane is rather naive—uncharacteristically so—on the subject of Blanche.

As you read on, you might find it interesting to look for evidence for and against Jane's opinion on this topic. What does Mr. Rochester himself have to say about Blanche? What do other people, such as Mrs. Fairfax, think of her? How is Blanche's flirting with Rochester different from Jane's own "unconventional" conversations with him. Jane obviously thinks there is a big difference.

One afternoon a few days later, the guests are waiting for Mr. Rochester to return from an errand when a tall, well-dressed stranger appears at the door. He's Mr. Richard Mason, who says he's an old friend of Rochester's from Jamaica, in the West Indies.

While Mr. Mason is waiting in the drawing room, a servant announces another unexpected visitor. An old gypsy woman has come to the house, demanding to tell the ladies' fortunes. Blanche thinks this sounds like fun. One by one, the ladies take turns going into the library where the gypsy woman is waiting. All of them emerge giggling—except for Blanche Ingram,

who has obviously heard something that upset her
very much.

CHAPTER 19

Now it's Jane's turn to have her fortune told. Jane
finds the gypsy wearing a red cloak, a wide-brimmed
hat that hides her face, and smoking a pipe. Not very
impressed, she compares the woman unfavorably to a
Sybil—a prophetess from classical mythology. The
gypsy tells Jane that she is going to read her fortune
by studying the shape of her head.

NOTE: The belief that a person's character was
revealed by the shape of his or her skull—called phre-
nology—was prevalent in the mid-19th century. In an
earlier scene (Chapter 14) Jane has already analyzed
Mr. Rochester from the shape of his forehead.

The gypsy questions Jane at length about her feelings for Mr. Rochester and the rumors of his engagement to Miss Ingram. Since the gypsy mentions in
passing that she's a friend of Grace Poole, Jane
becomes wary and avoids saying how she really feels
about Rochester. In a long and rather flowery speech,
the gypsy then tells Jane that her eyes are "full of
feeling" and her mouth meant to know laughter, but
the shape of her forehead shows self-respect—it
seems to say, "I can live alone . . . I need not sell my
soul to buy bliss."

By the end of this speech, Jane realizes that the gypsy is speaking in the voice of—Mr. Rochester!

Very pleased with himself, Mr. Rochester removes
his disguise and asks Jane whether he didn't do a
wonderful job of imitating a gypsy. Jane is not
charmed, however. She tells him that it was very
unfair of him to try to trick her. Silently, however, she

is congratulating herself for having managed to get through the interview without saying anything embarassing.

Suddenly Jane remembers to tell Rochester about the arrival of Mr. Mason. Rochester is staggered by the news. He tells Jane that he wishes he could be far away with her on some island, away from danger. And he asks her, mysteriously, whether she would still be his friend even if it meant defying society.

She answers cautiously that she would remain true to any friend who deserved her loyalty.

CHAPTER 20

Once again Jane is awakened during the night—this time not by laughter, but by an agonized scream.

The scream wakes everyone in the house, but only Jane has heard the cries for help coming from the room directly above her own. Mr. Rochester says a servant had a nightmare, and he sends the rest of the household back to their rooms. Jane, however, gets dressed, guessing that he is going to need her help. Sure enough, he returns in a few minutes and leads her to one of the locked rooms on the third floor. There Jane finds Mr. Mason, his face white as a corpse's and one arm soaked in blood.

Rochester asks Jane to nurse Mr. Mason while he goes for a doctor. Before leaving, however, he warns Mason and Jane that they are not to speak to each other, no matter what happens.

Jane hears the unearthly laughter of Grace Poole in the next room, and she hardly knows what she's more afraid of—that Grace will manage to break through the door and attack again or that Mr. Mason will die before Mr. Rochester returns. When the doctor comes, he discovers that, besides the stab wounds, there are teeth marks on Mr. Mason's shoulder. "She bit me," Mr. Mason mutters. "She sucked the blood; she said she'd drain my heart."

This frightening revelation convinces Jane that Grace Poole is a monster. But she's still puzzled. Why does Mr. Rochester keep a woman like Grace in the house? And why does he seem to be afraid of Mr. Mason?

As soon as Mason can be moved, he is hustled out a side door of the house. He'll be cared for by Carter, the doctor, until he is well enough to leave England.

Rochester calls Jane to come out into the garden, and they wander down a quiet walk to an ivy-covered alcove. Jane tries to question him about the night's events. His answers aren't very satisfactory. He repeats that he won't feel safe until Mr. Mason is out of England and then talks vaguely about how a man can be haunted all his life by an error of his youth. What if such a man found a "gentle, gracious stranger" who could bring him peace of mind? Rochester asks. Would he be justified in joining his life to hers, even if it meant going against custom?

Just what is Mr. Rochester talking about? Is he suggesting that he might marry Blanche—a woman some might consider too young for him. Or is he hinting at something even more daring—such as marriage to a mere governess? Notice that Jane never tells us in so many words exactly what *she* thinks Mr. Rochester has in mind. In any case, her answer avoids the issue. She tells Rochester that no man should depend on another human being for his entire happiness. He should look to God instead.

At this, Mr. Rochester turns sarcastic. He suggests that he may be marrying Miss Ingram after all and even asks Jane whether she would be willing to sit up with him on the night before his wedding.

CHAPTER 21

Jane tells us as this chapter begins, that she believes in "presentiments," "sympathies," and "signs"—that is, premonitions, mental telepathy, and omens. It isn't too surprising when, after Jane dreams of a baby—an omen of family trouble—Bessie Leaven's husband shows up at Thornfield with the news that John Reed has commited suicide. Mrs. Reed has suffered a stroke and is demanding to see Jane. In spite of her vow never to visit Mrs. Reed again, Jane asks for a week's leave in order to answer the dying woman's request.

Jane receives a chilly welcome from Mrs. Reed's two daughters. Eliza is pale and thin, and wears a "nun-like" crucifix around her neck. Georgiana is plump and overdressed, and she inspects Jane's dull brown traveling dress with a disapproving sneer. Jane has heard earlier from Bessie that Georgiana was about to elope with an army officer when Eliza spoiled the plan by warning Mrs. Reed. It soon becomes clear to her that the girls not only hate each other, they hate their mother too, and are waiting impatiently for the old woman to die.

It would be natural to suppose that Mrs. Reed has sent for Jane because she is sorry for the way she treated her in the past and wants to ask for forgiveness. Nothing of the kind! Even when she's delirious, the very name "Jane Eyre" sets Mrs. Reed raving about how much she hates the girl. The only reason she has asked for Jane, Mrs. Reed finally reveals is that she's afraid to die without confessing another wrong she did Jane just three years ago; Mr. John

Eyre, Jane's uncle, sent Mrs. Reed a letter saying he wanted to adopt Jane, bring her to Madeira, and make her his heir. The thought of the niece she hated having such good luck was too much for Mrs. Reed, so she told him that Jane died during the typhus epidemic at Lowood School. In the end, of course Jane does forgive the dying Mrs. Reed.

NOTE: Reading this scene you may find yourself thinking back to Jane's days at Lowood, when Helen Burns kept advising her to learn to forgive her enemies. Helen's philosophy seemed impossibly idealistic to Jane, at the time. Now that she is older, however, she finds it easier to understand Mrs. Reed's faults. She no longer has power over Jane's life; she is a troubled old woman, and Jane cannot bring herself to hold a grudge.

Jane stays on at Gateshead for a whole month, helping Georgiana and Eliza to plan for their futures after their mother's death. Georgiana and Eliza are almost caricatures; their useless lives illustrate the fates of so many single women in Victorian society. Georgiana thinks of nothing but parties; lazy and bored by day, she spends most of her time lolling on the sofa. Eliza, who is about to convert to the Roman Catholic church, is busy every minute with her religious observances, yet we can't help feeling that Eliza's religion is just something she throws herself into because it fills up an otherwise empty existence.

NOTE: You will have to decide for yourself whether the portrait of the Reed sisters is a fair one. Notice that Jane Eyre, through her interest in painting and drawing, is able to fill usefully the empty hours that weigh so heavily on the two sisters. So perhaps

Charlotte Brontë is trying to make a point here about the need for women to have useful and creative work. On the other hand, you'll find that this author rarely has a good word to say about young women from the upper classes of society. Do you think this is of prejudice, or is it her realistic outlook on such women's way of life?

CHAPTER 22

The 100-mile coach trip from Gateshead back to Thornfield takes Jane two days.

Jane didn't write ahead to tell Mrs. Fairfax when she was coming back, and she decides to leave her trunk at the station in Millcote village and walk the last few miles to Thornfield. On her way to the house, she surprises Mr. Rochester, who is seated in the meadow, writing. Rochester exclaims that Jane's unexpected arrival is another proof that she's an elf. Hearing that Mrs. Reed has died, he says of Jane: "She comes from the other world—from the abode of people who are dead. . . . " Jane, for her part, can't help feeling delighted that Rochester has obviously missed her.

But Jane's happiness at being back at Thornfield is clouded by the prospect of Mr. Rochester's forthcoming marriage. He tells Jane that he has just ordered a fine new carriage for the use of the future Mrs. Rochester, presumably Blanche Ingram.

NOTE: Rochester comments that his bride will look like Queen Boadicea in the new carriage—a double-edged compliment. Boadicea was the warrior queen who fought against the Romans during the first century B.C., and Mr. Rochester seems to be hinting that married life with Blanche Ingram promises to be less than peaceful.

Jane knows that if Rochester does marry Blanche, Adèle will be sent away to school and she'll have to find a new job. She tries to prepare herself to leave Thornfield, but over the next two weeks she can't see any evidence that the wedding is actually being planned. Mr. Rochester isn't even bothering to visit the Ingrams, who live less than 20 miles away. Little by little, Jane allows herself to hope that the marriage is not going to take place after all.

By now, she can't deny to herself that she is very much in love with Mr. Rochester.

CHAPTER 23

It is Midsummer Eve.

NOTE: This holiday, celebrated on June 23, is associated with the supernatural. Unlike Halloween, whose theme is ghosts and the world of the dead, Midsummer Eve is a time when otherwise sensible people fall foolishly in love. There is also a superstition that on this night young women can find out whether or not their lovers have been true to them.

Shortly after sunset, Jane is walking in the orchard when she smells the aroma of Mr. Rochester's cigar. Not trusting herself to be alone with him, she tries to make her way back to the house. But Rochester catches up with her. He tells Jane that the time has come to give her notice; he has found a new position for her with a family in Ireland, the O'Galls. Jane breaks down in sobs at the news, admitting that she loves Thornfield and is filled with "terror and anguish" at the prospect of parting from Mr. Rochester forever.

At this, Rochester's mood changes completely. He tells Jane that he no longer thinks about marrying Blanche and only told Jane he did in order to shock her into revealing her true feelings for him. "I have no bride!" he exclaims, and drawing Jane close, kisses her passionately on the lips.

At first Jane thinks Rochester is proposing an affair. And then, when he begins to talk about marriage, she thinks that he is making fun of her.

"Am I a liar in your eyes?" Rochester asks, offended.

You may recall that this is the same charge that was leveled at Jane earlier in the story by Mrs. Reed and Mr. Brocklehurst. Jane, faced with Rochester's insistent declarations of love, begins to think that Rochester must be sincere.

Rochester goes on to tell Jane that he never really cared for Blanche Ingram and that, in order to test her love for him, he spread the rumor that he was not nearly as rich as he seemed to be. After that Blanche's interest in marriage had cooled considerably.

Now completely reassured, Jane admits that she has been in love with Rochester all along. The two of them embrace again. For the first time she calls him by his first name—"Dear Edward!" He calls her "my little wife." "Come to me—come to me entirely now," he says.

But suddenly, just when everything seems to be resolved between the lovers, Rochester becomes very troubled. "God pardon me!" he exclaims as he holds Jane close to him, "and man meddle not with me. . . ."

Jane is confused. Who would want to interfere with their love?

Suddenly a shadow blocks out the light of the moon and a roaring wind races through the meadow. A loud crack of thunder startles Jane, and she burrows her face against Rochester's shoulder. Then the rain starts to pour down, forcing the lovers to run back to the house for shelter. The storm rages fiercely for two hours.

The next morning Jane learns that a bolt of lightning struck the venerable old horse-chestnut tree in the orchard, splitting its trunk in two. Remember that Jane has told us she believes in omens and premonitions. The chestnut tree struck by lightning must be an omen—but of what? Is it a sign of the unleasing of the lovers' passion? Or does it warn that God is displeased with their union?

CHAPTER 24

The next morning, the sky is clear and all seems calm and beautiful again. "Nature must be gladsome when I was so happy," Jane tells herself.

Mr. Rochester, meanwhile, is filled with plans for their approaching marriage. He tells Jane he wants to take her traveling in Europe after the wedding, and he urges her to come into town with him and let him buy her some expensive new dresses, which she will need when she is elevated to the position of a rich man's wife.

In this chapter, Rochester tries to tell Jane that, despite their unequal social status, she has the upper hand emotionally. "You please me, and you master me—you seem to submit. . . . [yet] I am conquered," he tells Jane.

Jane is not quite so confident. She is troubled by her total financial dependence on the man she loves. She won't take the fancy dresses he wants to buy her and accepts only two modest ones in their place. She tells him that she doesn't want to be in the position of a kept woman or mistress, and she insists on continuing to behave as a governess until after the wedding.

NOTE: How do you feel about Jane's decision? Is she being foolish to refuse to accept presents from her own fiancé? Or do you think she has sound reasons for holding on to at least a facade of independence? Perhaps she thinks too little of herself to be able to accept presents lavished on her?

CHAPTER 25

A month has gone by and it's now the day before the wedding.

Mr. Rochester has been away overnight on business, visiting some farms he owns in a nearby district. On his return, he tells Jane that they will be leaving on their wedding trip one hour after the ceremony.

Jane has something more troubling on her mind. She tells Rochester that on the previous night she suffered a terrible nightmare. Thornfield Hall was in ruins, and she was running away from it carrying a baby in her arms.

NOTE: Remember, from Chapter 21, that Jane believes this dream foretells trouble in the family.

But the worst was yet to come that night. Jane awakened to find a strange woman in her room. The woman was large and tall, with dishevelled black hair and a horrible, discolored face—blotchy skin, swollen lips, and bloodshot eyes. As Jane watched in fear, this strange woman placed Jane's wedding veil over her own head, studied herself in the mirror, and then angrily ripped the veil in two parts and trampled them underfoot. Then she came to Jane's bed and leaned over to stare at her.

Jane swears that she never saw this horrible-looking woman before. It wasn't Grace Poole. The woman reminded her of something unreal—of "that foul German spectre—the Vampyre."

Rochester tells Jane that she must be imagining things. Of course it was Grace Poole! Who else *could* it be? He promises that after he and Jane have been married for a year and a day he will explain why he continues to keep "such a woman" in his house. In the meantime, he urges Jane to spend her last night at Thornfield on the couch in Adèle's room.

NOTE: Would you be satisfied with this explanation? Probably not. Rochester sounds a little bit like one of those ladies' men who is always urging naive young girls to "trust me." On the other hand, his promise that he will answer Jane's questions after "a year and a day" of marriage sounds like a fairy tale, not real life. If you're willing to see *Jane Eyre* as a real-life fairy tale—at least in part,—then you may understand why Jane doesn't insist on getting the answers about Grace Poole *before* the wedding. And yet, in real life, most people take an awful lot on faith when they fall in love and decide to get married. This is especially true for a girl like Jane who has no experience with sex and romantic love.

CHAPTER 26

Jane and Rochester have planned a private wedding, with no guests or attendants. But as they arrive at the small country church, Jane is slightly curious about two strangers lingering in the churchyard; she feel sure they'll come into the church. Sure enough, they do.

The ceremony begins and when the minister asks, "Will you take this woman . . ." one of the strangers speaks up. "The marriage cannot go on: I declare the existence of an impediment."

This a favorite dramatic scene in romantic novels, movies, and TV soap operas. But you'll seldom, if ever, see this moment followed by a more dramatic revelation.

The stranger who spoke identifies himself as Mr. Briggs, a London solicitor (lawyer). And now the other man emerges from the shadows to reveal that he is—Mr. Richard Mason. Mr. Briggs reads a document confirming that Mr. Rochester was married fifteen years earlier to a Miss Bertha Mason of Spanish Town, Jamaica—Mr. Mason's sister! Not only is the first Mrs. Rochester still alive, but she can be found at this very moment at Thornfield Hall!

At first, the minister refuses to believe this story. He's never heard of a Mrs. Rochester at Thornfield. But Mr. Rochester breaks down and admits that every word of Briggs's accusation is true. His wife Bertha, now totally insane, is the hideous woman who sneaked into Jane's room two nights earlier. She is also the woman who attacked Mr. Mason. Grace Poole is a servant hired as a guardian for Bertha.

Rochester insists that the minister, the church clerk, Mr. Briggs, and Mr. Mason return to Thornfield with him and Jane to see Bertha for themselves. He takes them into the locked room on the third floor. At once, the madwoman leaps for Mr. Rochester and tries to strangle him. She is a big woman and maniacally powerful, but Rochester manages to subdue her with some gentleness. "That is *my wife*," he tells his visitors bitterly.

NOTE: There's very little humor in *Jane Eyre*, but it makes a rather unexpected appearance in this scene. Asked how her patient is doing, Grace Poole replies mildly that she is well but feeling "rather snappish"—a laughable understatement.

Before leaving Thornfield, Mr. Briggs informs Jane that he's been acting as the agent of her long-lost uncle in Madeira, Mr. John Eyre, who is now too ill to travel. After Jane had written to tell him about her marriage, Mr. Eyre, who knew Richard Mason, decided the wedding had to be stopped in order to save his niece from the disgrace of a bigamous marriage.

After the visitors leave, Jane rushes to her own bedroom and bolts herself in. She is devastated—a "cold, solitary girl again" who sees all her hopes for the future in ruins. However, even in despair, Jane can't bring herself to put the blame on Rochester. "I would not say that he betrayed me," she comments. Her greatest fear, in fact, is that Rochester didn't really love her after all, and that he only chose her because he dared not try to make an illegal marriage with a woman who was his social equal.

CHAPTER 27

That afternoon, Jane decides that she must leave Thornfield at once.

Rochester pleads with her to stay. He begs for forgiveness, and he asks Jane to come with him to his villa in the south of France. No one there will know that they aren't legally married. He'll shut up Thornfield Hall and leave Grace Poole there with "that fearful hag."

NOTE: Divorce is never mentioned. Under the law at that time, a man couldn't divorce an insane wife.

Jane tells him he mustn't hate his wife just because she's mad. That not why he hates her, he says; does Jane think he would hate her if she were mad? "I do, indeed, sir," she replies.

He tells her she's wrong, and he explains why he feels the way he does about his wife. Whether or not you find his story convincing, it's certainly a dramatic one. He tells Jane that he never loved Bertha Mason and hardly knew her at the time of their marriage fifteen years ago. He was rushed into the wedding by his own father and by the Mason family, who managed to conceal from him the early symptoms of Bertha's condition. After the wedding Bertha turned out to be immoral, unintelligent, and a heavy drinker. Within four years she was completely mad. At this point, Rochester decided to commit suicide. He was standing with a pistol to his head when "true Wisdom" suggested another plan—he would take his wife back to Thornfield to be cared for while he traveled in Europe.

Jane seems satisfied with Rochester's answer, but you may not be. We feel sympathy for Rochester being tricked into marriage, but he doesn't really say anything that could make Jane believe he wouldn't also hate her if she went mad. Jane's worry is one that occurs to all of us at one time or another. What would happen if illness, or some other calamity beyond our control, made us unlovable? Would the people who love us now still feel the same way about us? Would our families still feel a duty to take care of us? The story has a lot to say about this subject, but it never does answer Jane's question in so many words. You will have to decide for yourself how you feel about Rochester's attitude toward Bertha.

Next, Rochester apologizes for being too cowardly to tell Jane the truth about Bertha. He had been afraid that "instilled prejudice" would prevent her from overlooking his legal marriage. "I should have appealed to your nobleness," he says. Grabbing her around the waist and devouring her with "a flaming glance," he once more begs her not to leave him.

Jane is tempted. Why not run away with Rochester? What could be more important than making the man she loves happy? "Who in the world cares for you?" she asks herself—no one will be injured by what she does. And then she has her answer: "*I* care for myself," she declares. "The more solitary, the more friendless, the more unsustained I am, the more I will respect myself. I will keep the law given by God; sanctioned by man."

Jane cannot be swayed. She will leave Thornfield and Mr. Rochester forever.

NOTE: No doubt some of you will be very disappointed by Jane's choice. Is it really the law of God that keeps her from running away with Mr. Rochester, or just the divorce laws of England? And is the fear of sin Jane's only concern? Perhaps she's also afraid that Rochester will grow tired of her or lose his respect for her. Some readers find in Jane's answer a hint that if she had money of her own, or a social position equal to Rochester's, her decision might have been quite different. Others believe she is truly following her own idea of what's right. What do you think?

That night, Jane dreams that she is a child again and her mother is urging her, "My daughter, flee temptation!" She wakes before dawn and steals out of the house.

CHAPTER 28

When she left Thornfield, Jane had only 20 shillings. She hails a passing coach on the road and asks the driver to take her as far as her money will carry her.

After two days, Jane's money runs out. The driver leaves her at a crossroads in the moor district. Jane spends the night sleeping outdoors under the stars, and in the morning she hikes into the village where she asks without success for work as a house servant or a seamstress. By the end of the day she's so hungry she begs for a piece of bread from a farmer; the next day it's a meal of porridge from a child who is about to feed the cold mess to a pig.

Jane returns to the moors, planning to spend a second night out of doors, but the threat of rain sends her looking for a sheltered spot. At that moment she notices a light in the distance. She follows this beacon until she finds herself standing outside a neat little house. Peeking through a window, she sees an elderly woman servant and two young ladies. The latter are translating a story in a strange language (it turns out to be German).

NOTE: At first, Jane thinks the distant light is a ignis fatuus. Also known as "elf-fire" or "will o' the wisp," this is a phosphorescent glow that sometimes occurs around marshes and is caused by decaying plant matter.

Jane knocks at the door of the house. The servant woman, suspicious that Jane might be fronting for a band of house robbers, refuses to let her in. But she's saved by the arrival of the young ladies' brother, St. John (pronounced sĭn'jŭn). He welcomes Jane into the house, where he and his sisters give Jane supper and a room for the night. Afraid that news of the scandal at Thornfield might reach even this remote place, Jane decides to give them a false name—Jane Elliott.

CHAPTER 29

Worn out by her wanderings on the moor, Jane is ill for three days. When she recovers, she learns from the old servant, Hannah, that the lovely house where she is staying is known as Marsh End or Moor House. It is owned by the two young ladies, Mary and Diana Rivers, whose father has recently died. St. John Rivers, their brother, is a minister with a parish in the village, which Jane now learns is called Morton.

Left alone with St. John in the parlor, Jane notices that he is in his late 20s, with blue eyes, blond hair, and the handsome features of a classical Greek statue. In spite of his gentle looks, Jane can't help sensing that there is something "restless, or hard, or eager" in St. John's nature. Jane admits that she is a governess who once attended Lowood School, but she refuses to tell St. John her real name or where she's been living. His sisters take her side, and he agrees to help her find work.

CHAPTER 30

In the meantime, Jane stays on with Diana and Mary. She quickly becomes fond of the sisters, who are not only kind and cheerful but have a lively interest in books and learning. St. John is another story. He strikes Jane as cold and withdrawn, always lost in his own thoughts. Only when she hears St. John preach a sermon in church does Jane catch a glimpse of a more fiery side to his nature.

A month goes by. Diana and Mary are getting ready to go back to their jobs as governesses with two fashionable and wealthy families. Jane gathers her courage to ask St. John whether he has found any work for her. In reply, St. John tells Jane about a charity school for poor children in Morton village. The school is supported by a Miss Oliver, the daughter of a wealthy factory owner. St. John has been teaching a class of boys. Would Jane be interested in teaching the girls?

The job St. John offers Jane is a step down from being a governess. She'll have to live very simply, and she won't have any chance to use her education in French and drawing. Her students will be just beginning to learn to read and write. After only a moment's thought, Jane decides to accept. At least she will have her independence.

St. John, however, predicts that Jane will not stay in Morton very long. You are "impassioned," he tells Jane. "Human affections and sympathies have a most powerful hold on you." He confesses that even he, a Christian minister, has felt restless and longed to escape the sleepy village of Morton.

Jane hardly knows what to think of this confession. She is even more confused when Diana and Mary hint that when they leave for their jobs again they may be saying good-bye to St. John for the last time. Sobbing, Mary tells Jane that she has tried and failed to talk her brother out of his "severe decision."

Before Jane can find out what that decision is, St. John comes back into the room carrying a letter. He reads out the news that their "Uncle John" is dead. Both he and the girls are disappointed to learn that their uncle, who quarreled with their father long ago, has left most of his money to another relative, who is unknown to them.

CHAPTER 31

On her first day as a charity school teacher, Jane is forced to keep reminding herself that her coarsely clad pupils are human beings, as good as the children of any aristocrat.

NOTE: As much as Jane hates the social snobbery of people like Blanche Ingram, she has strong prejudices of her own. To her credit, she recognizes this fault and tries to overcome it. Decide for yourself how well she succeeds.

St. John visits Jane's modest cottage and encourages her to stay with the job. He tells her that it is possible to conquer one's natural desires through willpower, and to "turn the bent of [one's own] nature." By way of illustration, St. John confides that he has recently passed through a crisis of his own. Only a year earlier, he had come to the conclusion that he had made a mistake by entering the ministry. He was longing for a career in literature, politics, the army— anything that would offer more excitement than his religious duties. But after much soul searching, he has decided that his restlessness was a message from God, calling him to the life of an overseas missionary.

Now, adds St. John, he has only "one last conflict with human weakness" to overcome before he is ready to leave for the orient.

At that moment, their conversation is interrupted by the arrival of Miss Oliver, the young heiress whose money supports St. John's school. Jane is taken aback to discover that Rosamond Oliver is not only breathtakingly lovely, but also very obviously in love with St. John. It's not hard to guess the nature of St. John's conflict.

CHAPTER 32

Jane's nights are still filled with dreams of Mr. Rochester. But her days are satisfying. She finds that some of the "heavy-looking, gaping rustics" in her classroom are actually turning out to be good students, and she feels that she's well liked in the neighborhood.

In the meantime, she has been learning more about Rosamond Oliver. Jane decides that Rosamond, though somewhat shallow, is a basically cheerful and good hearted person. Perhaps more important, Jane visits Rosamond's home, Vale Hall, and learns that Mr. Oliver would be very happy to see his daughter marry St. John. A self-made man, whose fortune is from his needle factory, Mr. Oliver is attracted to the idea of his daughter marrying into an old, upper-class family like the Rivers's. He doesn't care a bit that they are no longer wealthy. It occurs to Jane that by marrying Rosamond, St. John could make himself happy, and by putting Rosamond's money to good use, still accomplish as much as he would in a lifetime of missionary work.

To sound out St. John's feelings, Jane shows him a portrait she's drawn of Rosamond. St. John admits that he loves Rosamond "wildly," but he is also convinced that he would soon be sorry if he married her. Rosamond would not make a good missionary's wife.

Why not give up the idea of becoming a missionary, Jane suggests.

St. John won't listen. He assures Jane that although he seems distraught over giving up Rosamond, he will soon forget her. He is more cold-hearted than Jane thinks, he insists.

NOTE: From the way St. John talks about Rosamond, you might well suspect that he's giving her up *because* he loves her. Do you think he's the kind of person who feels he *must* sacrifice his happiness in order to serve God? Or does St. John enjoy punishing himself? Is he afraid of love and sex? Or too self-centered to commit himself to a relationship with another human being? All we know for sure is that St. John is too confused to fully understand his own motives.

While St. John is looking at Rosamond's portrait, he notices something on the blank sheet of paper Jane uses to protect the painting. He's visibly startled. Jane doesn't know why, but she sees him tear off a corner of it and slip it into his glove—then he quickly leaves.

CHAPTER 33

The next evening, in the middle of a driving snowstorm, St. John pays Jane a surprise call. She sees at once that he's got something serious on his mind. After a long silence, St. John begins to tell Jane a story about a poor orphan girl who lived with a family named Reed, was sent away to Lowood School, and eventually fell in love with a man named Rochester . . .

Jane's first reaction is that St. John has brought her some bad news about Mr. Rochester. Nothing of the kind!—he hasn't heard anything about Rochester. He's had a letter from Mr. Briggs, John Eyre's solicitor, who's been looking for Jane all over England. Mr. Eyre has died and left her a fortune of 20,000 pounds—enough to make her a rich woman for life. St. John goes on to explain that it was only when he noticed Jane's signature on the cover of her portrait that he realized that Jane Elliott—as she had called herself—was the same person as the missing heiress Jane Eyre.

Naturally, Jane is overjoyed by her unexpected inheritance. Only after the news has taken a few minutes to sink in does she begin to wonder how St. John managed to get a letter from Mr. Briggs, confirming the amount of the legacy, in such a short time. Reluctantly, he confesses that Briggs had written to St. John even before he guessed Jane's identity. John Eyre is the same "Uncle John" whose death we heard about in Chapter 30! And St. John, Mary, and Diana are Jane's cousins—the children of her father's only sister. Jane immediately decides that she will split her fortune four ways, giving equal shares to St. John and his sisters.

NOTE: In a story filled with improbable coincidences, this is surely the most improbable of all. Not only does Jane's uncle know Richard Mason and learn about Jane's wedding in time to stop it . . . not only does he leave his money to a niece he has never seen . . . we're now supposed to believe that he's also related to the Rivers family, people Jane met purely by chance!

If you're the kind of reader who wants stories to be true to life, this string of coincidences might spoil the

story for you. On the other hand, if you believe in
omens, as Jane does, you may believe that something
more than chance sent Jane to the door of the Rivers
cottage.

CHAPTER 34

The money from Mr. Eyre makes it possible for
Jane, Diana, and Mary to give up teaching and set up
housekeeping together at Moor House.

NOTE:　　At one time or another, all of us daydream about what we'd do if we were rich. Some
readers think that Diana and Mary are idealized portraits of Charlotte Brontë's sisters, and that the way of
life they lead in this chapter is a kind of wish-fulfill-
ment fantasy—Brontë's own dream of having
enough money so they could all live at home together.
Happiness for Diana, Mary, and Jane means freedom
from having to work for a living and the pleasure of
just being together. St. John, it's true, tells Jane, "You
have only worked for a few months!", and he hopes
that she'll soon put her talents to use again. But Jane
replies that she's perfectly happy just to live at Moor
House.

Modern girls reading this will think, "That's not a
very exciting dream!" Most of you are probably planning to have careers. But in Victorian times, women
didn't have careers. They were supported—by their
husbands if they were lucky enough to get one, or by
their families if not. If they worked, it was out of abso-
lute necessity. They didn't have a whole lot of choice
in jobs, and they couldn't make very much money.

Meanwhile, Rosamond Oliver has finally given up
on St. John and announced her engagement to another man. St. John pretends to be happy about this

news. He tells Jane that giving up Rosamond was a
"victory" over his sensual desires. Jane finds this hard
to believe.

Nevertheless, Jane agrees to help St. John study
Hindostanee (Hindi), the language he'll be using in
his missionary work. Studying side by side with him,
she gradually comes to appreciate his better qualities—patience, dedication, and a burning desire to do
some good in the world. By the time summer comes,
and St. John proposes that they marry and go to India
together, Jane may be ready to consider the offer. You
may well find this surprising. Why would Jane be
willing to go off to spend her life in a strange country
with a man she does not even like? The reasons Jane
gives are she has no idea what has become of Mr.
Rochester and needs to make some kind of decision
about her future. She will probably never have another chance to marry. But are these reasons good
eno gh? Reading between the lines, you may notice
that Jane's feelings about St. John are more complicated than she cares to admit. Perhaps she feels guilty
about not doing anything useful with her life. Or, perhaps, for all her seeming independence, Jane may be
secretly attracted by the idea of marrying a man who
wants to dominate her.

St. John doesn't make it easy for Jane to say yes. He
tells her plainly that he's offering a loveless marriage.
"I claim you—not for my pleasure," he says, but for
God's service. This is too much for Jane. She answers
that she will go to India with St. John as his coworker,
but not as his wife.

St. John turns her down. His practical excuse is that
it wouldn't be proper for him to take a 19-year-old
single girl to live in India. The situation would be sure
to cause gossip and misunderstandings. Jane, however, suspects that this isn't the real reason. It occurs to

her that St. John won't be happy until he has complete control over her life.

NOTE: Sadism and masochism weren't subjects that could be discussed openly in 19th-century novels. But if you read carefully, you may find hints that the author is trying to say that St. John has sadistic tendencies. For example, he tells Jane that if she won't marry him, God would regard her going to India as a "mutilated sacrifice." What kind of man would use language like this in trying to get a woman to marry him?

The way St. John talks in this scene may also remind you of Mr. Brocklehurst—another clergyman who seemed to enjoy seeing the poor suffer. When *Jane Eyre* was first published, some readers were shocked by the way it portrayed ministers of God. Charlotte Brontë was accused of writing an "anti-Christian" book. Today, some readers would say that the novel is very religious in spirit—and that it only criticizes those who pretend to do good, but without love in their hearts. You will have to decide for yourself whether the view of organized religion in *Jane Eyre* is a fair one.

Before leaving Jane, St. John quotes a line from a poem by Sir Walter Scott: "Looked to river, looked to hill." We're not sure what he means by this, but it reminds us that Jane is torn between St. John (whose last name is Rivers) and Mr. Rochester, whose mansion Thornfield is set on hilly ground. Rochester offered Jane love, but without marriage. St. John offers marriage, and with it the useful and socially respectable position of a missionary's wife, but it is an offer made without love.

CHAPTER 35

St. John delays his departure for a week. He hopes to get Jane to change her mind, but his coldness and air of repressed hostility only make Jane more determined to refuse him. St. John's attitude is that by refusing to marry him, Jane has not only rejected him personally but refused to do God's will. When St. John repeats his proposal of marriage, Jane recognizes, in a flash of insight, that not only does St. John not love her—he subconsciously wants to make her suffer, as he has suffered in giving up everything to follow what he believes is God's will. "You almost hate me," Jane tells him accusingly. "If I were to marry you, you would kill me. You are killing me now."

St. John still does not give up, and Jane repeats her offer to go to India as his assistant.

Although St. John doesn't even pretend to be in love with Jane, he is insulted by her answer. Turning "lividly pale," he remarks that he isn't interested in having a "female curate" (assistant minister). He wants a wife. However, he offers to arrange for Jane to go out to India with a married couple.

Jane says no. She only considered going to India in the first place out of a "sisterly" desire to help St. John, and she reminds him that she feels no duty to go with strangers, especially since she feels sure she wouldn't live long in that tropical climate. St. John can't believe that this is the real reason. He accuses her of still harboring a "lawless and unconsecrated" love for Mr. Rochester. Jane admits that this is so.

Nowadays, St. John's goal of converting India to the Church of England would be somewhat controversial. (Many people still think of missionary work as a noble calling; others feel there's something condescending about it—that it means you don't think other cultures are as good as your own.) You won't find this debate in *Jane Eyre*, but the novel does pose a more general question: Which is more important, changing the world or concentrating on personal relationships? In this section of the story, Jane seems to be torn between the two goals. But notice that as soon as St. John is out of the picture she has no interest in missionary work at all. Some readers point out that her decisions at critical points like this show that Jane Eyre, for all the talk about her passionate nature, is a very conventional heroine who can't imagine happiness except in the role of a traditional wife. Others defend Jane for insisting on finding a way of life that is right for her. There's no right solution to this debate, but your opinion one way or the other will influence your judgment of Jane.

Diana Rivers approves of Jane's decision, reminding Jane that St. John would be sure to work her as hard as he works himself and saying that Jane is much too good a person to be "grilled alive in Calcutta."

However, that same evening, as St. John leads Jane, Diana and Mary in family prayers, Jane almost changes her mind. Although he's cold and almost repellent in his personal dealing with her, St. John is an inspiring speaker on the subject of religion. Listening to him pray, Jane is impressed by his sincerity and his zealous desire to do God's work. "I was tempted to cease struggling with him," Jane tells us, "to rush down the torrent of his will into the gulf of his existence, and there lose my own."

By this time Diana and Mary have gone to bed, leaving Jane and St. John alone. Jane tells St. John that she could decide now to marry him, but only if she can be sure that it's truly God's will. "Show me, show me the path!" she cries out to heaven.

In her over-excited state, Jane thinks she hears a voice in the distance. It is not God's voice, however, but that of Rochester calling her name in anguish. "Where are you?" Jane calls out. But the only answer is the sound of her own voice echoing off the hills.

Suddenly, Jane feels strong again. Very much in control, she sends St. John home and retires to her room to pray alone—not under St. John's influence this time, but on her own.

CHAPTER 36

The next morning, Jane finds a note from St. John telling her that he'll return two weeks later, just before leaving for India to see if she is ready to make a decision in his favor. But the voice Jane heard the night before, real or imaginary, has shown Jane what she must do. She leaves Moor House that same day to return to Rochester.

Jane can hardly wait to see Thornfield again. But she is in for a terrible shock. The mansion is in ruins. Nothing remains but a charred wreck, overgrown with weeds.

Back at the inn, the innkeeper tells Jane the story of Thornfield's destruction.

After Jane left, Mr. Rochester fell into a deep depression. Adèle was sent away to boarding school, and Mrs. Fairfax (who has not known the secret of Bertha Mason) retired on a generous pension. Grace Poole remained to take care of Bertha. But it seems that Grace was given to drinking too much gin— which was why Bertha had been able to escape when she set fire to Rochester's bed and frightened Jane in her room.

One night, about two months after Jane's departure, Grace Poole fell into an especially deep, drunken stupor, and Bertha got out again. This time, she went into the room that had belonged to Jane and set the bed on fire. Fortunately, Mr. Rochester awakened in time to warn the servants and get them out. But when he ran back into the burning house to rescue Bertha, she ran out onto the roof. Witnesses saw Rochester trying to pull her to safety, but she leaped to her death from the burning battlements. Minutes later, the roof collapsed in flames. Rochester survived, but with horrible wounds. He lost one eye, became blind in the other, and had his left hand amputated.

Since that time, the innkeeper tells Jane, Rochester has been living as a hermit at Ferndean, a manor house about 30 miles away. Jane immediately hires a carriage to taker her there.

CHAPTER 37

Ferndean is a roomy but sparsely furnished house buried deep in the woods, which Mr. Rochester's father had bought to use as a hunting lodge. Jane arrives just before dark, and after paying off her driver, walks the last mile through the dense forest on foot. As she comes near the house, she sees Rochester standing on the front steps, obviously blind and helpless. She longs to rush forward and greet him with a kiss.

NOTE: Does this scene remind you of another fairy tale? What about *Sleeping Beauty*? In this version, however, it is the woman who has arrived to rescue her "sleeping prince."

Jane convinces Rochester's servant to let her carry in the glass of water he's asked for. Rochester, though blind, recognizes Jane's voice and is overjoyed. He tells her that he has often imagined her "dead in some ditch" or an "outcast among strangers" and blamed himself. On the contrary, Jane tells him, she is now independently wealthy, thanks to her Uncle John Eyre. She offers to be Rochester's neighbor, nurse, and housekeeper—to take care of him from now on. "It is time someone undertook to rehumanise you," she says.

Of course, what Jane really wants is to be Rochester's wife, but she's not sure whether he wants her, given his present condition. And he, in turn, is afraid to ask her for fear of being turned down.

The next morning, listening to the story of her life at Moor House, Rochester cannot help showing his jealousy of St. John. Jane teases him into admitting that he still loves her. At this, Rochester tells Jane that he is a "ruin of a man," like "the old lightning-struck chestnut tree in Thornfield orchard." Would Jane think him foolish if he still wanted a wife in spite of this?

Jane replies sensibly that her feelings would depend on whom he wanted as a bride. Choose *"her who loves you best,"* she urges. He tells her he will choose *"her I love best."*

Rochester then asks Jane to marry him, and she gladly accepts. She dismisses his suggestion that marriage to a blind, one-handed man will be a sacrifice. If "to press my lips to what I love best" is a sacrifice, she says, then she delights in it.

Finally, Rochester tells Jane that he now knows he was wrong to try to trick her into a bigamous marriage. He is no longer bitter about losing his sight, and his sufferings have reconciled him with God. Only a few days ago, on Monday evening, he says, he prayed to God for Jane's return and called her name aloud. A voice answered, and he knew it was Jane's.

Hearing this story, Jane realizes that it was on Monday night, at the very hour Rochester called out to her, that she heard his voice crying her name at Moor House. Jane decides to keep her knowledge of this "inexplicable coincidence" to herself. Her reunion with Rochester is already a profound and moving experience in its own right—and the role of the supernatural in bringing them back together is something that she would prefer to ponder in private.

CHAPTER 38

"Reader, I married him." So, with this much-quoted line, begins the conclusion of the novel. In this final chapter, we are reminded that the voice we have been hearing narrate the story all along belongs to the mature Jane Eyre, who is recalling events that happened years earlier.

We are now brought up to date on what took place in the ten years following Jane and Rochester's marriage: Adèle, Rochester's little French ward, was taken out of her strict school and placed in a more lenient one where she was able to grow up free and cheerful. Diana and Mary Rivers both found good husbands.

As for Jane and Rochester, their marriage is a complete success. ". . . I am my husband's life as fully as he is mine. No woman was ever nearer to his mate than I am," Jane says.

After two years of marriage, Rochester even regained the sight of his one remaining eye—and in time to see the face of his first-born son.

The story ends on a note of forgiveness for St. John. Hard labor and tropical diseases have already taken their toll on St. John's health, but St. John feels no fear at the prospect of an early death which will reconcile him with God at last and end his struggles with earthly temptations.

A STEP BEYOND

Tests and Answers

TESTS

Test 1

1. The Brontë sisters wrote under pen names _____
   because
   A. there was a prejudice against women
      novelists
   B. their father didn't want them to write
      novels
   C. they wanted to seem mysterious

2. Charlotte Brontë made Jane Eyre plain _____
   because
   A. she felt readers would sympathize with her
      more that way
   B. she herself was plain
   C. it was the literary fashion to have ugly
      heroines

3. One of Jane Eyre's main faults is that she is _____
   A. cold and unloving
   B. desperate to marry a rich man
   C. rebellious and passionate

4. In contrast to Jane, who fulfills herself by _____
   working, we see unhappy idleness in
   A. Blanche Ingram
   B. Eliza and Georgiana Reed
   C. Mary and Diana Rivers

5. An example of a Byronic hero in this book   _____
   would be
   A. John Reed
   B. Edward Rochester
   C. St. John Rivers

6. A positive view of religious faith is shown in   _____
   the character
   A. Mr. Brocklehurst
   B. St. John Rivers
   C. Helen Burns

7. An important element running through this   _____
   book is
   A. hints of the supernatural
   B. political statements about woman's roles
   C. the healing power of nature

8. Jane's daily life at the Reeds' house is   _____
   miserable because
   A. her cousin John hits her
   B. no one loves her or takes her side
   C. she sees a ghost

9. The "red room" is   _____
   A. a room in the Reed house where Jane is
      shut up for punishment
   B. the room at the school where Helen Burns
      dies
   C. the room at Thornfield Hall where Grace
      Poole is locked away

10. Lowood School gets better because   _____
    A. Miss Temple learns Jane is not a liar
    B. a typhus epidemic reveals the unhealthy
       conditions to the public
    C. Jane becomes one of the teachers

11. The theme of *Jane Eyre* is the search for love. Discuss.

12. The concept of duty is very important to the heroine, Jane Eyre. Discuss its meaning for her.

13. George Henry Lewes, who was a leading critic of Charlotte Brontë's own time, wrote of *Jane Eyre:* "Reality— deep, significant reality—is the great characteristic of the book." Others, with equal confidence, describe the novel as romantic. What elements of realism and romanticism do you find in the novel? Discuss.

14. *Jane Eyre* is told in the first person by a single narrator— and from one point of view. This *could* be monotonous, or too limited. Discuss one or more narrative devices that Charlotte Brontë uses to vary the pace or broaden the point of view of the story.

15. "[Jane's] perceptions about Thornfield are constantly used as foreshadowings of what she is about to discover of its master."—Robert Bernard Martin (see Further Reading). Discuss.

Test 2

1. Jane at first thinks Mrs. Fairfax is the lady of ——— Thornfield because
   A. she knows so much of the family's history
   B. she acts so grand
   C. Jane herself is so naive

2. Jane immediately takes to Mr. Rochester ——— because
   A. he has a lively imagination
   B. he is handsome
   C. he loves Adèle Varens

3. Rochester immediately takes to Jane because ———
   A. she is modest and shy
   B. she is a talented painter
   C. she is proud and independent

4. At Thornfield, in the middle of the night, a _____
   violent visitor comes to I. Rochester; II.
   Richard Mason; III. Jane Eyre
   A. I only
   B. II and III only
   C. I, II, and III

5. Mr. Briggs is working for _____
   A. Jane's Uncle Reed
   B. Jane's Uncle John Eyre
   C. Jane's cousin St. John Rivers

6. Rochester believed his marriage wasn't a real _____
   marriage because
   A. he wasn't warned that Bertha was insane
   B. he only married Bertha for her money
   C. he loves Jane more than he loves Bertha

7. Rochester's first wife came from _____
   A. Paris
   B. Jamaica
   C. Madeira

8. When Jane learns that Rochester is already _____
   married, he offers to
   A. divorce his wife for Jane
   B. take Jane as his mistress
   C. marry Blanche Ingram instead

9. Jane is willing to go to India with St. John _____
   Rivers because
   A. she needs to earn a living
   B. it would force him to marry her
   C. she wants to do good work

10. The five "acts" of *Jane Eyre* take place in these _____
    settings:
    A. Lowood, Thornfield, Gateshead, Moor
    House, Ferndean

    B. Ferndean, Lowood, Thornfield, Gateshead, Moor House

    C. Gateshead, Lowood, Thornfield, Moor House, Ferndean

11. Jane Eyre is an amateur artist. What function does her interest in drawing serve in the story?

12. Describe the structure of *Jane Eyre*.

13. "Conventionality is not morality," wrote Charlotte Brontë in her preface to *Jane Eyre*. Yet many readers feel that Jane Eyre's idea of what is moral always agrees with conventional middle-class standards. Discuss.

14. Weather is very important in *Jane Eyre*. Discuss.

15. "The real innovation of Charlotte Brontë is that she writes fiction from the point of view of an individual and not from the point of view of society in general."— Bruce McCullough (see Further Reading). Discuss.

    What are Jane Eyre's views on social classes? In what way does she capture truths about society that more objective writers might miss? How is her viewpoint limited?

ANSWERS

Test 1

1. A   2. A   3. C   4. B   5. B   6. C

7. A   8. B   9. A   10. B

11. Remember that more than one kind of love is important in the novel. There's romantic love. There's the love of God, expressed in its pure form by Helen Burns, and with more psychological complexity in the character of St. John Rivers. There's also self-love, or self-respect. Jane finds happiness only when she is able to reconcile all three. Finally, don't overlook the word *search* in the

question. What actions does Jane undertake to further her search? How does her understanding of love change over time?

12. You could approach this question by discussing the characters who remind Jane of her duty at one time or another. How are these characters described? What influence does each one of them have over Jane? Don't neglect to talk about St. John. Why does he have such a strong influence over Jane for a time? And why does she conclude that it is not her duty to marry him?

    You could also answer this question by discussing Jane Eyre's concept of *marital* duty. What are the duties that a wife owes a husband, and vice versa? Do you believe Jane at the end when she denies that her marriage to Rochester has involved a sacrifice on her part?

13. Most readers agree that the character of Jane is *realistic*. She is poor, plain, friendless; and she has all the everyday problems that go with her situation as a governess. When a rich man falls in love with her, her troubles are by no means over. Other characters, too, are seen preoccupied with everyday pursuits—teaching school, learning German, baking pies, looking for rich husbands. Effectively or not, most are presented in terms of a balance of good and bad qualities.

    Obvious elements of *romanticism* in the novel include the use of supernatural elements, the ongoing mystery of Bertha Mason, and the intensely personal point of view. Emphasis on the importance of the imagination, an interest in childhood experiences, and the search for independence and individual fulfillment are also characteristic of romanticism.

14. Here are some examples of narrative devices: overheard conversations; Jane's retellings of her own dreams; digressions in which Jane addresses the reader directly;

stories told to Jane by other characters (such as the inn-keeper's tale in Chapter 36); and the interjection of rel-evant quotations from books, poetry, and songs.

15. Here are a few examples: The very physical description of Thornfield (Chapter 11) with its stolid gray exterior and grove of "mighty old thorn trees, strong, knotty and broad as oaks" predicts Rochester's solid, unhand-some appearance and thorny character. When she first sees the third story of the house, Jane observes that its old-fashioned furniture make it a "shrine of memory," and later we learn that Rochester's past is literally present there in the person of Bertha. In Chapter 25 Jane dreams of Thornfield as a ruin and sees herself falling from a "narrow ledge" or "wall," as Rochester later does when the roof collapses in the fire. Later, Jane sees the actual wreckage of Thornfield before she finds the crippled Rochester himself.

Try to find some other examples in which the house takes on a symbolic importance.

Test 2

1. C 2. A 3. C 4. C 5. B 6. A
7. B 8. B 9. C 10. C

11. The child Jane Eyre uses the romantic illustrations in *History of British Birds* as a trigger for escapist fantasies. The drawings she does at Lowood serve a similar func-tion, as Rochester notices when he comments on their "elf-like," dreamy character (Chapter 13). Later, Jane paints one portrait emphasizing her own plainness and another of beautiful Blanche Ingram as an exercise in self-discipline. When she revisits the Reeds at Gates-head (Chapter 21), her sketching is a constructive way to fill the idle hours that weigh so heavily on Georgiana and Eliza. At Moor House, she uses her portrait of Rosamond Oliver to draw out St. John about his feel-

ings, and it is from her signature on a portrait that he learns Jane's identity.

Here are some points to think about: Why are Jane's most carefully done portraits of Blanche and Rosamond, women she doesn't especially admire? What is her attitude toward physical beauty? What's the meaning of the sketch of Rochester that she makes in Chapter 21? What does it mean that (in Chapter 38) she becomes the "eyes" of her blind husband?

12. The structure of the novel follows, chronologically, the personal development of its central character, Jane Eyre. Beyond this, there is no single "right" answer.

You might base your discussion on the "five-act play" structure of Robert Bernard Martin, showing how each new locale (Gateshead House, Lowood, Thornfield, Moor House, and Ferndean) corresponds to a stage in Jane's inner quest. In this case, pay particular attention to the journeys that link the sections.

Or you could make a different breakdown. For instance, try dividing the story into three parts: Jane's childhood, her stay at Thornfield, and her growth to maturity at Moor House and after.

13. One starting point for a discussion could be Jane's reasons for deciding to leave Thornfield in Chapter 27. Notice that she says then: "I will keep the law given by God; *sanctioned by man*." Isn't her goal always to make a respectable marriage? Or you might want to consider why Jane returns to Thornfield when she does. How can she forgive Rochester for lying to her and yet accuse St. John of trying to "kill" her by the kind of marriage he offers?

14. "Nature must be gladsome when I was so happy," Jane thinks when she wakes to a "brilliant June day" on the morning after Rochester's proposal. Be as specific as you can be about the language used to describe weather

and its relationship to the mood of various scenes. For example: the crimson sunset and icy cold of her first meeting with Rochester; the "sky of steel" (Chapter 15) under which Rochester tells the story of Céline; the lovely spring morning (Chapter 20) when Rochester offers Jane a "half-blown rose" and tells her he thinks he has found a "cure" for his dissipation; the lightning storm on the night he proposes.

Some other questions to think about: Why is the weather particularly beautiful in Chapter 5 when Helen Burns lies dying? What's the significance of the weather during the night Jane sleeps outdoors on the moors (Chapter 28): at night there is the "pure" sky and "kindly" star overhead; on waking the next morning she finds a "perfect day" and a "golden desert" illuminated by sunshine.

15. You may choose to argue that Brontë presents a very vivid and realistic portrait of the situation of a governess, precisely because it is so personal. Don't forget Jane's prejudices about the "French defects" of her pupil Adèle and her "coarse" students at Morton school. Remember also the views of governesses expressed by others—the complaints of the Ingrams and Rochester's deprecating comments on governesses who play the piano "a little," but not well.

On the other hand, you might want to talk about Jane's ideas about wealth. Jane considers herself rich when she has five thousand pounds. Rochester is rich, too, and so is Rosamond Oliver. How much information does the novel give us about the different ways of life associated with varying amounts and kinds of wealth? Does Jane understand the problems of the rich, or does she simply equate money with freedom?

Term Paper Ideas

1. Here are four different views of *Jane Eyre*. Choose one and defend your view: (a) *Jane Eyre* is basically a religious novel, about the need for God and His influence on our behavior; (b) *Jane Eyre* is basically a feminist novel, about the emotional equality of men and women; (c) *Jane Eyre* is basically a romantic novel, outlining a young girl's fantasy of a masterful lover; (d) *Jane Eyre* is basically an "apprenticeship" novel, about the universal experiences of growing up.

2. How do Jane's dreams function in the novel? How do they generate suspense and foreshadow the future? How do they advance the story?

3. Compare the opinions about Jane expressed by Bessie Lee and Miss Abbot.

4. Why does Mrs. Reed dislike Jane so much? Is Jane partly at fault? Do you find Mrs. Reed's treatment of Jane believable?

5. Many readers have commented that the color red is used in the novel to signify passion. Discuss. Or limit your discussion to the imagery of fire, or of blood.

6. In what sense is Thornfield a haunted house?

7. Why does Rochester often accuse Jane of bewitching him? Do his reasons for saying this change over time?

8. Is Rochester a "flesh-and-blood" hero or is he, as Virginia Woolf suggested, "a portrait drawn in the dark"? Defend your view.

9. In what ways is Rochester a Byronic hero? In what ways is he not? Base your discussion on a biography of Byron and/or a discussion of Byronic qualities, such as the one

found in Moglen's *Charlotte Brontë: The Self Conceived* (see Further Reading).

10. Compare Rochester to the character of Heathcliff in Emily Brontë's *Wuthering Heights*.

11. In Chapters 27 and 37, Rochester is compared to Samson. Why? You'll find the Biblical story of Samson in Judges 13-16; also look at *Samson Agonistes* by John Milton.

12. Jean Rhys' *The Wide Sargasso Sea* tells the story of the first Mrs. Rochester from her own perspective. Choose one character in *Jane Eyre*—such as Bertha, Rochester, Blanche Ingram, or Mrs. Reed—and write a story from his or her point of view.

13. What is Charlotte Brontë's attitude toward marrying for money? Is she against it under all circumstances? Why does Jane Eyre inherit money before her reconciliation with Rochester?

14. Many nineteenth-century novelists were preoccupied with the subject of the "marriage market." Compare Brontë's attitude toward the connection between love and money with the views in one of the following: *Vanity Fair* by Thackeray; *Pride and Prejudice* by Jane Austen, *Dombey and Son* by Dickens.

15. How does Brontë use the character of Grace Poole to generate suspense? What does Jane learn about Grace from Mrs. Fairfax? From Rochester? From her own observation? In what sense does Grace turn out to be a dangerous person after all?

16. Analyze the role of coincidence in the plot. How do coincidences advance the story? How do they make possible Jane's spiritual and moral development? Are some coincidences so unbelievable that they interfere with your enjoyment of the story? Why or why not?

17. Discuss the description of Rosamond Oliver in Chapter 31. Does the language suggest that there's something trite or insipid about Rosamond's type of beauty? If so, does this contradict the admiration explicitly expressed by Jane? Do you think the author intended a contradiction, or does this section show that Brontë's style was uncontrolled?

18. How are the moors described in Chapter 28? What does their wild beauty mean to Jane? Some readers think this chapter was inspired by a poem by William Wordsworth called "Guilt and Sorrow"; you might choose to base your analysis on this comparison. Or contrast Charlotte's description with Emily's description of the moor in *Wuthering Heights*.

19. Rochester often compares Jane to a little bird; later, in Chapter 37, he is compared to a "caged eagle." What's the meaning of this bird imagery? Can you find other places where it occurs?

20. What's the significance of the chestnut tree struck by lightning?

21. In what ways is *Jane Eyre* a Cinderella story?

22. In what ways is Jane Eyre a feminist version of *Sleeping Beauty?*

23. Indentify and discuss one or more selections in the novel where Jane tells us something about herself that makes us more likely to trust her judgment about other people and about events.

24. What do you think of St. John Rivers? Can you make a case defending his character? Is it possible that Jane was wrong about his coldness, or prejudiced against him because she was still in love with Rochester? Or was he as bad, or worse, than Jane says?

25. If you can find a copy of Winifred Gerin's biography of Charlotte Brontë (See Further Reading), read the description of Cowan Bridge school and the Reverend Carus Wilson. Discuss how Brontë turned them into Lowood and Mr. Brocklehurst. Was she writing an accurate description, as she claimed? Or was her picture of the school colored by the emotions of childhood?

26. Some readers think Charlotte Brontë has no sense of humor. Others think that when humor does occur in *Jane Eyre* it is clumsy and heavy-handed. Some find the conversations between Jane and Rochester witty and amusing. Choose one view and defend it with specific examples.

27. How did Charlotte Brontë go about dividing the story into chapters? Do you notice a certain pattern? How does she use suspense to make you want to move on from one chapter to the next?

28. When it comes to the supernatural, *Jane Eyre* sometimes seems to be trying to "have it both ways." The mood depends on our being frightened and/or impressed by supernatural happenings, yet the author never tries to make them truly convincing or believable in a literal sense. (See Jane's comments on Rochester's crying out to her in Chapter 37). Do you ever think this is unfair? Or do you think it makes the novel more effective?

29. Many light romantic novels have been written that copy the story and mood of *Jane Eyre* to one degree or another. The best known of these is *Rebecca* by Daphne Du Maurier. You might be interested to see how the two books are alike, and how they differ. Which heroine do you think is more interesting?

Further Reading

CRITICAL WORKS

Basch, Françoise. *Relative Creatures: Victorian Women in Society and the Novel.* New York: Schocken Books, 1974. Contains a useful chapter on "Revolt and Duty in the Brontës."

Bentley, Phyllis. *The Brontës and Their World.* New York: Viking Press, 1969. An illustrated look at the places and people associated with the Brontë sisters' lives and works. Bentley is also the author of a good short biography of the Brontë sisters.

Cecil, David. "Charlotte Brontë" in *Early Victorian Novelists.* Chicago: University of Chicago Press, 1958, pp. 100–135. Although he admires some aspects of *Jane Eyre*, Cecil concentrates on the novel's weaknesses.

Craik, W.A. *The Brontë Novels.* London: Gethuren, 1968. Defends the characterizations of Rochester and St. John.

Ewbank, Inga-Stina. *Their Proper Sphere: A Study of the Brontë Sisters as Early Victorian Female Novelists.* Cambridge: Harvard University Press, 1966.

Gaskell, Elizabeth Cleghorn. *Life of Charlotte Brontë.* New York: E.P. Dutton, 1908. An early biography by a woman writer who was a close friend of Charlotte Brontë. Well worth reading, even though not all of Mrs. Gaskell's facts and opinions are accepted today.

Gerin, Winifred. *Charlotte Brontë: The Evolution of a Genius.* Oxford: Clarendon Press, 1967. The most complete and thoroughly researched biography of Charlotte.

Gilbert, Sandra M., and Susan Gubar. *The Madwoman in the Attic. A Study of Women and the Literary Imagination in the Nineteenth Century.* New Haven: Yale University Press, 1979.

Gregor, Ian, ed. *The Brontës: A Collection of Critical Essays.* Englewood Cliffs, N.J.: Prentice-Hall, 1970. A good source book.

Knies, Erik A. *The Art of Charlotte Brontë.* Athens: Ohio University Press, 1969.

McCullough, Bruce. "The Subjective Novel" in *Representative English Novelists.* New York: Harper & Brothers, 1946, pp. 169–183. Sees *Jane Eyre* as an example of romanticism.

Martin, Robert Bernard. *The Accents of Persuasion: Charlotte Brontë's Novels.* New York: W.W. Norton, 1966. Very useful on imagery, the supernatural, and the religious and moral themes of the story.

Moglen, Helene. *Charlotte Brontë: The Self Conceived.* New York: W.W. Norton, 1976. Good on the Byronic hero and the fairytale aspects of Brontë's novels.

O'Neill, Judith, ed. *Criticism on Charlotte and Emily Brontë.* Coral Gables, Florida: University of Miami Press, 1979.

Ratchford, Fannie E. *The Brontës' Web of Childhood.* New York: Russell & Russell, 1964. An interesting look at how Charlotte Brontë's childhood fantasies and writings influenced her mature novels.

Showalter, Elaine. *A Literature of Their Own: British Women Novelists from Brontë to Lessing.* Princeton, N.J.: Princeton University Press, 1977. A perceptive feminist critique.

Thorslev, Peter L. *The Byronic Hero.* Minneapolis, Minn.: University of Minnesota Press, 1962.

Tillotson, Kathleen. "Jane Eyre" in *Novels of the Eighteen Forties.* London: Oxford University Press, 1965.

Winnifrith, Tom. *The Brontës.* New York: Macmillan, 1977.

Woolf, Virginia. *A Room of One's Own.* New York: Harcourt, Brace & World, 1957. (Originally published in 1929.)

AUTHOR'S OTHER WORKS

_____. *Shirley*. London: Oxford University Press, 1969. A tale of love and social unrest, set in England during the Napoleonic era.

_____. *The Professor*. London: Oxford University Press, 1967. Brontë's first novel, not published until after her death, tells the story of an English schoolmaster in France who must choose between a well-to-do woman and the young student teacher he loves.

_____. *Villette*. Boston: Houghton Mifflin, 1971. Besides *Jane Eyre*, the only Charlotte Brontë novel still much read today. The novel draws on Charlotte Brontë's experiences in Belgium; its heroine Lucy Snowe, is in some ways a darker more complex version of Jane Eyre.

Shorter, Clement. *The Brontës: Life and Letters*. 2 vol. New York: Haskell House, 1969. Charlotte Brontë's letters are filled with illuminating insight into the art of *Jane Eyre* as well as the author's own life. (Note: There are several other editions of the letters, and you will also find selections from them in a number of biographies and critical studies.)

Glossary

Barmecide Feast   An unsatisfying meal. The phrase comes from a story in the Arabian Knights about a Persian nobleman who served an imaginary meal to a begger.

Bluebeard   A character in a French fairy tale who married and murdered one wife after another.

Boadicea   A warrior queen of ancient Britain who led a revolt against the Romans.

Bridewell   A prison.

Cadeau   The French word for gift.

Corsair   A pirate.

Croquant   French for eating or crunching on. The expression, used by Rochester, comes from the verb croquer, meaning to crunch.

Cuyp-like   Resembling a painting by Cuyp, a Flemish painter known for peaceful rural scenes.

Dian   (spelled Diana in some editions) The goddess of the hunt. Blanche Ingram is said to have a figure like Dian. Normally this would be a compliment, but notice how often Blanche is compared to women who have some military or predatory function.

Eutychus   A man who fell asleep while listening to a sermon by St. Paul and tumbled out of an open window.

Heath   A wild shrub with pink or purple flowers; heather is one variety of heath.

Juggernaut   An idol representing the Hindu deity Krishna. Once a year the idol was pulled through the streets in a cart and devout worshippers supposedly committed suicide by throwing themselves under the cart's wheels.

Madeira   An island in the Atlantic Ocean about 400 miles west of Morocco.

Moor   An area of open land not good for farming.

Rasselas   A philosophic romance by Samuel Johnson. A young man named Rasselas searches the world for the secret of happiness and concludes that happiness lies in being content with one's lot.

Rizzio, David   An Italian musician in the court of Mary Queen of Scots. Thought to be the Queen's lover and involved in a plot to murder one of her husbands.

Sybil   One of a group of women in ancient Greece believed to have the power to see into the future. Usually spelled Sibyl.

Tyrian-Dyed   Purple in color. The name comes from the ancient Middle Eastern city of Tyre, which was famous for the royal purple dyes produced there.

Vulcan   The Roman god of fire and metal-working. Vulcan was portrayed as a cripple and this is the characteristic Rochester has in mind when he compares himself to the god in Chapter 37.

Wolfe, James   A British general who died while trying to capture Quebec from the French in 1759. The death of Wolfe, mentioned in Chapter 11, was a very common subject for patriotic paintings.

The Critics

Jane Eyre was an immediate success with the reading public and has remained popular ever since. The first critics, too, were mostly favorable.

One exception was a reviewer named Elizabeth Rigby, who condemned the novel as profoundly immoral and "anti-Christian"—not so much because of Mr. Rochester's character as because of Jane's "unregenerate and undisciplined" spirit.

Far more typical was the reaction of the great critic George Henry Lewes (who, like Rochester, had left his first wife to live with another woman, the novelist George Eliot):

> Reality—deep, significant reality—is the great characteristic of the book. It *is* an autobiography— not, perhaps, in the naked facts and circumstances, but in the actual suffering and experience. . . . This faculty for objective representation, is also united to a strange power of subjective representation. We do not simply mean the power over passions—the psychological intuition of the artist, but the power also of connecting external appearances with internal effects—of representing the psychological interpretation of material phenomena.

Writing in 1925, the novelist Virginia Woolf praised the highly personal quality of Charlotte Brontë's art:

> The writer has us by the hand, forces us along her road, makes us see what she sees, never leaves us for a moment or allows us to forget her. At the end we are steeped through and through with the genius, the vehemence, the indignation of Charlotte Brontë. Remarkable faces, figures of strong outline and gnarled feature have flashed upon us in passing; but it is through her eyes that we have seen them.

David Cecil, in his *Early Victorian Novelists*, makes perhaps the best case against Charlotte Brontë's writing. His charges against Brontë include:

- lack of restraint
- lack of a sense of humor
- thin, two-dimensional characterizations

But, most of all, Cecil attacked Brontë's improbable plot:

> . . . . Not one of the main incidents on which its action turns is but incredible. It is incredible that Rochester should hide a mad wife on the top floor of Thornfield Hall, and hide her so imperfectly that she constantly gets loose and roams yelling about the house, without any of his numerous servants and guests suspecting anything: it is incredible that Mrs. Reed, a conventional if disagreeable woman, should conspire to cheat Jane out of a fortune because she had been rude to her as a child of ten: it is supremely incredible that when Jane Eyre collapses on an unknown doorstep after her flight from Rochester it should be on the doorstep of her only surviving amiable relations.

David Cecil was rather typical of his generation in feeling distaste at Brontë's "naive" and overemotional approach to her art.

But during the last several decades, many critics have praised Brontë for the very qualities Cecil disliked:

> . . . . If in Rochester we see only an Angrian-Byronic hero and a Charlotte wish-fulfillment figure (the two identifications which to some readers seem entirely to place him), we miss what is more significant, the exploration of personality that opens up new areas of feeling in sexual relationships.

. . . . Charlotte's remoulding of feeling reaches a height when she sympathetically portrays Rochester's efforts to make Jane his mistress. Here the stereotyped seducer becomes a kind of lost nobleman of passion and specifically of physical passion.

> —*"Charlotte Brontë's New Gothic," by Robert H. Heilman, reprinted in O'Neill,* Critics on Charlotte and Emily Brontë

"Jane Eyre is at bottom . . . largely a religious novel, concerned with the meaning of religion to man and its relevance to his behavior. Jane discovers at Lowood that she can comprehend religion only when it has some relation to man, but at Thornfield she sees the opposite error, of man attempting to remake religion to his own convenience."

> —*Robert Bernard Martin,* The Accents of Persuasion

Madness is explicitly associated with female sexual passion, with the body, with the fiery emotions Jane admits to feeling for Rochester. In trying to persuade her to become his mistress, Rochester argues that Jane is a special case: 'If you were mad,' he asks, 'do you think I should hate you?' 'I do indeed, sir,' Jane replies, and she is surely correct' . . . When they finally marry, they have become equals, not only because Rochester, in losing his hand and his sight, has learned how it feels to be helpless and how to accept help, but also because Jane, in destroying the dark passion of her own psyche, has become truly her "own mistress."

> —*Elaine Showalter,* A Literature of Their Own

And finally, in defense of Brontë's "unrestrained" style:

> On the first page of *Jane Eyre* the first issue raised is in fact the issue of style. The wrong style, in girlhood and in language, is the reason why Jane is kept by Mrs. Reed from joining the other children around the fire.
>
> —*Ellen Moers*, Literary Women